Aponavicius*

(AH-pah-NAH-vih-chus)

From BC Superfan to Walk-On Kicking Phenomenon

by M.B. Roberts

story editor: Brian Reidy

COVER DESIGN:
Marjie Parsons, www.DigiRetouch.com

*This book is meant to inspire young athletes everywhere.
Mostly, it's to let people know that
when your chance comes, you've got to be ready.
So get ready.
Your overnight success is due anytime.*

About the Author:
M.B. Roberts is the author of seventeen books including
Reflections of the Game: Lives in Baseball,
Bear's Boys: 36 Men Whose Lives were Changed by Coach Paul Bryant
and
The Great Book of NASCAR Racing Lists.

"Steve Aponavicius has been compared to Rudy but the difference is he actually played and made a huge impact on the BC program. He truly lived a Hollywood story."
— *Jon Meterparel, Voice of the Boston College Eagles*

"His story is second to none in college football."
— *Matt Ryan, NFL Quarterback*

Contents

Unless otherwise noted, all photos are courtesy of
the Aponavicius family.

Introduction

The Kicker

Who in their right mind would want to be a kicker? Most of the time, the fans and even the kicker's own teammates barely know he exists. Then, a critical moment arises. Maybe the clock is winding down, the game is tied and a field goal would win it. Suddenly, all eyes are on the guy who boots the ball and after just one play, he will be either the hero or the goat.

Steve Aponavicius compares the job of kicker to the left-handed relief pitcher in baseball.

"You come in, then you go off and you're done," he said. "But kicks win and lose games. The third phase of the game – kicking—is just as important as offense or defense. And sometimes, it's all on the shoulders of a short, skinny, former soccer player."

Talk about pressure. In the course of a successful field goal or extra point, just 1.2 seconds elapse from snap to kick. In just over a second, the kicker must connect with the ball, get it off the ground and send it through the uprights or it will be blocked by really big players that nobody, least of all the lowly kicker, wants to end up underneath. Everything has to work perfectly, from the snap to the hold to the kick itself. It's a precision thing.

Kickers aren't machines. Unforeseen factors often come into play – the wind, the rain, the snow, the crowd, the turf, the kicker's fragile psyche – and as a result, there have been some incredibly memorable missed kicks over the years.

One of the most infamous botched kicks in pro football history was attempted by Garo Yepremian on January 14, 1973, during Super Bowl VII. The Miami Dolphins were leading the Washington Redskins 14-0 with just two minutes left to play when Yepremian stepped onto the field to attempt the field goal, which would all but set the win in stone. But then, Redskins defensive end Bill Brundige blocked the kick. Yepremian got to the ball before any other player but rather than falling on it to stop the play, incredibly, he attempted a pass!

Unfortunately, the kicker only managed to bat the ball into the air and it landed in the waiting hands of Redskins cornerback Mike Bass, who returned the ball forty-nine yards for a touchdown.

Despite the scare, the Dolphins won the Super Bowl and preserved their perfect season of 1972.

Yepremian, who was already a star kicker, went on to have a fantastic career. He was voted Kicker of the Decade 1970-1980 by both *Sports Illustrated* and the Pro Football Hall of Fame, which will certainly induct him as a member someday. But people remember the big misses.

No one knows that better than former Buffalo Bills kicker Scott Norwood. Despite being a major contributor to the Bills' talented offenses of the late 1980's and early 90's, Norwood is often remembered as the guy who cost his team the win in Super Bowl XXV when he missed a forty-seven yard field goal as the clock ran out. People forget he was the Bills' all-time leading scorer (a record formerly held by O.J. Simpson), until he was surpassed by his successor, Steve Christie, in 1998, but people tend to remember Al Michaels saying, "No good! Wide right!"

Then there's Doug Brien. Jets fans are still mad about his two field goal misses from the 2004 AFC Divisional Playoff game against the Pittsburgh Steelers. True, both kicks were potential game-winners and he did miss twice. But do people remember that when he retired after playing in 136 games, he was one of the most accurate kickers in NFL history? (80.9%) How many fans know that he once kicked thirty-four straight field goals of less than forty yards?

The kicks they miss always cancel out the ones they hit. This is not news to Redskins kicker Graham Gano, who recently booted a clean fifty-yarder in the fourth quarter which would have won the September 19, 2010, game against the Texans, had their head coach not called time-out a split second before the play began.

The classic attempt to ice the kicker worked. After the time-out, Gano kicked again and shanked it right. The field goal was no good and the Texans won in overtime. Sometimes missed kicks aren't the kicker's fault. Just ask Tony Romo who botched the snap during a last minute attempt at a field goal, which would have given the Dallas Cowboys a playoff win against the Seattle Seahawks in 2007. Romo, already a Pro Bowl-bound quarterback, caught the ball cleanly but fumbled it as he tried to place it down for Martin Gramatica's nineteen-yard kick. Romo had been holding for the kicker since the previous season, before he ever even threw a pass in the NFL. No one noticed that. Fans don't usually even see the holder. But they definitely notice when a hold goes bad, the kick never gets off the ground and the final score reads 22-21 in favor of the other team.

Of course fans also take note of the good kicks. Especially the really long kicks or the game-winners. Fans sprung out of their seats back in October of 1998 when the Denver Broncos' Jason Elam nailed a sixty-three yard field goal in his team's 37-24 win against the Jacksonville Jaguars. Elam's kick, which tied the nearly thirty-year-old record held by Tom Dempsey of the New Orleans Saints, was originally set up to be a fifty-eight yard attempt but then a delay-of-game penalty pushed back the ball five yards.

"Those goal posts look pretty skinny from back there," Elam told sportsillustrated.cnn.com. "I tried not to look at them much; it can be intimidating."

According to Elam, three-quarters of NFL kickers could hit a field goal of his record-tying range but common sense prevents most coaches from taking the risk, unless, like Dempsey's kick, the attempt is made as the clock runs out at the end of the game or the first half.

That said, a handful of pro players have kicked field goals of sixty yards or better. Matt Bryant (Tampa Bay) hit a sixty-two yarder in 2006. Sebastian Janikowski (Oakland) converted a sixty-one yarder in 2009. Morten Anderson (New Orleans) and Steve Cox (Cleveland) both hit sixty-yard field goals in 1991 and 1984, respectively.

In 1979, Philadelphia Eagles barefoot kicker Tony Franklin made other players wonder if they really needed shoes when he nailed a fifty-nine yarder. Ten years later, Pete Stoyanovich matched the fifty-nine yard mark, as did Steve Christie of the Bills in 1993 and Morten Anderson, this time playing for the Falcons, in 1995. (The latter three did in fact wear shoes).

Although field goals tend to be shorter in the college game than in the pros, college kickers have nonetheless notched their fair share of impressively long kicks. In fact, one college player is credited with the longest field goal on record.

When he was a junior at Abilene Christian University in 1976, Ove Johansson kicked a sixty-nine yarder during ACU's homecoming game win against East Texas State University. ACU was playing in the NCIA (National Association of Intercollegiate Athletics) at the time so the NCAA (National Collegiate Athletic Association) record stands at sixty-seven yards, a feat accomplished by three players: Russell Erxleben (Texas, 1977), Steve Little (Arkansas, 1977), and Joe Williams (Wichita State, 1978).

The high school record for longest field goal is debatable, partly because many games aren't videotaped. With no evidence, the length of the kick is impossible to verify. Also, high school rules vary from state to state. Some leagues or coaches in individual games will allow free kicks, where the kicker kicks from a tee without pressure from defenders, which gives him an undeniable edge. Still, high school players have hit some impressive marks over the years, notably the seventy yarder by Alan Saunders of Oregon-Clay High School in Oregon, Ohio, in 2008 and the sixty-eight yarder by Dirk Borgognone of Reno High School in Reno, Nevada, in 1985.

More recently, in October of 2010, a young female kicker named Alana Gaither of Firestone High School in Akron, Ohio completed a forty-three yard field goal.

No doubt about it. Long bombs are an integral part of the game and always exciting to watch. But more often, games are won courtesy of shorter kicks.

During the same 1970 game where he booted his record-setting sixty-three yard kick, Tom Dempsey, who incredibly was born without a right hand and no toes on his right (kicking) foot, also kicked an eight-yard field goal. Both kicks counted for the same amount -- three points. When it comes to kickers, consistency is king.

Jan Stenerud, who along with George Blanda and Lou "the Toe" Groza is one of only three kickers in the Pro Football Hall of Fame (and the only one who didn't also play another position), accomplished what he did by being consistent. Not to say that Stenerud didn't hit his share of mega-long kicks during his nearly twenty-year career. Especially when it came to kickoffs.

During his heyday with the Kansas City Chiefs in the late 1960's and throughout the 70's it became so commonplace for Stenerud's kicks to sail past the endzone and into the seats that kickoff returns by opponents of the Chiefs almost never happened. In fact, it was partly due to Stenerud that in 1974 the NFL moved the kickoff point backwards from the forty to the thirty-five yard line and moved the goal posts from the goal line to the end line to make field goals more challenging.

From the start, Stenerud was steadfast. In his first four seasons as a pro, he went 108 for 153, hitting seventy percent of his field goals. (The combined average in the AFL and NFL at the time was fifty-three percent). He also successfully converted 212 of 213 extra points during his first six years. It's no surprise he was voted into the Hall of Fame in 1991, his very first year of eligibility.

With Stenerud, like other standout kickers, it wasn't just what he did but how he did it. And Stenerud kicked it soccer-style.

Stenerud came from Norway and was part of a group of foreign-born kickers who played pro football in the U.S. in the 1960's and 70's, despite never having played gridiron football when they were growing up. Many of these players excelled in other sports (Stenerud came to Montana State University on a skiing scholarship), but they all played soccer. And when they came to America, they brought their style of kicking with them and literally changed the game.

Before the mid-1960's, place kickers in football ran straight up at the ball and kicked it with their toe. These days, almost every pro and college kicker approaches the ball at an angle and kicks it with the instep of the foot.

And we have Pete Gogolak to thank for that.

Gogolak was fourteen years old when his family fled Hungary following the Soviet invasion of 1956 and moved to the United States. Back in Hungary, he and his brother played soccer – there was no such thing as gridiron football – but his new school didn't have a soccer team.

Then, in his junior year of high school, the football team at Ogdensburg (N.Y.) Free Academy held a mass kicking try-out where every player and potential player on the team was asked to make a boot. Gogolak decided he had nothing to lose and showed up for the try-out.

When he hit the field to take his kick, Gogolak stood at a forty-five-degree angle to approach the ball. According to a giants.com story, he immediately noticed the strange looks he was getting.

"Everyone looked at me and said, 'Jeez, what's going on here,'" Gogolak said. "I'll never forget the expression on my holder's face. He said, 'Hey, Gogolak, in this country you line up straight. If you line up that way, you'll either hit it in the stands or hit me in the butt.'"

Well, he did neither. The kick was long and clean and Gogolak became a stand-out on his high school team. Next, he played football at Cornell University where he became the first soccer-style kicker in college.

In 1964, he was drafted in the twelfth round by the upstart Buffalo Bills of the American Football League (AFL) and introduced his "sidewinder" style of kicking to the pros. He was instantly successful, putting up 102 points his rookie season (one quarter of the total points scored by the Bills that year).

After two seasons, he became the first AFL player to cross over to the NFL –thereby igniting the merger of the two leagues --when he signed with the New York Giants in 1966. During his nine seasons with the Giants, Gogolak went on to become their all-time leading scorer (646 points) and holds the franchise record for most points-after-touchdown (PAT's) attempted (277), most PAT's made (268), most consecutive PAT's (133), and most field goals (126).

More than anything, Gogolak revolutionized place kicking by introducing a new style that increased the accuracy of most every kicker that tried it. Today, soccer-style kicking is the universal standard in football.

Back in the 60's, it didn't take long for others to follow Gogolak's lead. One of the first was his younger brother, Charlie Gogolak, who broke all NCAA records while kicking at Princeton and still holds the Ivy League record for the longest field goal of fifty-four yards.

In 1966, Charlie was drafted in the first round by the Washington Redskins and years before Eli and Peyton Manning were even born, the Gogolak brothers squared off against each other playing the same position for different teams when the Redskins beat the Giants in 1966 (72-41).

The Gogolaks paved the immediate way for other soccer-style kickers in the NFL, many of them foreign-born, including Jan Stenerud of Norway, Garo Yepremian of Cyprus and Toni Fritsch of Austria.

While soccer-style kicking became a lasting phenomenon, other placekicking trends failed to gain momentum. A prime example is barefoot kicking.

The short-lived trend came about in the late 1970's and early '80's and although there were very few players who kicked with no shoe, several were successful with the skin on pigskin approach. Arguably, the best known was Tony Franklin of the Philadelphia Eagles.

Franklin, who played college football (and kicked barefoot) at Texas A&M, grew up in Texas where the weather is hot and kids play football year round. With that in mind, it's not that difficult to understand why a young player would run around barefoot on a grassy field.

According to Franklin, it was a trial and error thing. He simply was able to kick the ball further without a shoe on his kicking foot. When he kicked for the Eagles, beginning in 1979, the fans accepted Franklin's shoeless quirk because he missed so few field goals. He also kicked a lot of long ones.

In fact, as a rookie, he booted a fifty-nine yarder in a crucial game against the division rival Dallas Cowboys, a kick that was the second-longest field goal in pro football history at the time. He went on to kick barefoot in Super Bowls for the Eagles and later, the New England Patriots.

There have been other barefoot kickers including Mike Lansford of the Rams and John Goodson, who punted barefoot for the Steelers. Rich Karlis of the Broncos went shoeless when he kicked the game-tying PAT as well as the game-winning field goal in the 1987 AFC Championship Game which sent his team to Super Bowl XXII.

Although kicking barefoot is almost universally banned in high school, it's still legal in the NCAA and the NFL. But mostly due to the development of thinner and more responsive shoes (and maybe those all-too lucrative shoe contracts?) the trend has definitely waned.

Although kickers don't always get the respect they deserve, at least over the years, placekicker, (PK), has become an actual, permanent position. This wasn't always the case.

In the early days of gridiron football, kicking duties were often performed by another position player who at some point or another showed the coach that he could kick. Prior to the 1960's, NFL teams didn't even hold a spot on their rosters for placekickers and punters. Other players would literally step in when needed. Over the years, some of the best kickers were also outstanding quarterbacks, running backs and linebackers.

Although they are also listed as kickers in the Pro Football Hall of Fame, Lou "The Toe" Groza and George Blanda were best known as a quarterback (Blanda) and as an offensive tackle (Groza). One of the five 2008 inaugural inductees into the American Kicking Hall of Fame, Jim Thorpe, was not only an Olympic Gold Medalist for track and field, but he was a football star who was a running back, defensive back, placekicker, and punter. But that was a long, long time ago.

These days, kicking is a more specialized duty. Most NFL teams employ placekickers and punters and unless someone is injured, rarely do they step in for each other. Some teams whittle things down even further, dividing up kickoff duty, place-kicking and punting.

Is it possible that despite the kicker's reputation as the redheaded stepchild of football, this often crucial position is garnering a bit of respect? After all, the game is called football.

There is probably no moment more exciting in sports than the last-second, football game-winning field goal. Kickers who miss such a kick experience the lowest of the lows. Kickers who make such a kick will never forget the thrill.

Maybe every player secretly longs to be the kicker. Even if it's just for one play. Evidently, Boston College's "Hail Flutie" quarterback, Doug Flutie, held just such a secret ambition and during the very last game of his NFL career, he finally got the chance to see it through.

Flutie spent his final season (2005) as the New England Patriots back-up quarterback behind Tom Brady. Some time before the last regular season game, ESPN announcer Chris Berman mentioned to Patriots Coach Bill Belichick that he'd seen Flutie drop kick the ball.

Evidently Flutie not only wanted to kick, he wanted to drop kick. Per the NFL rulebook, the skill was legal but had not been used since the Chicago Bears' Ray "Scooter" McLean converted a drop kick during his team's 37-9 championship victory over the New York Giants in December of 1941.

During the fourth quarter of a January 1, 2006 game against the Miami Dolphins, Belichick called in his backups. After number three quarterback, Matt Cassel, threw a touchdown pass, the number two quarterback, Doug Flutie, surprised everyone by jogging onto the field with the kicking unit.

After taking his position for a regular shotgun snap, which really confused the Dolphins, (Miami's Head Coach Nick Saban called a time-out to try to figure out what was happening), Flutie caught the ball, dropped it to the ground and when it bounced, kicked it through the uprights. By doing so, he not only made the extra point, but successfully completed the NFL's first drop kick in decades.

"I think Doug deserves it," Belichick told ESPN after the game. "He is a guy that adds a lot to this game of football, has added a lot through his great career—running, passing and now kicking."

Given the chance, who wouldn't want to kick it through those uprights? Maybe you aren't so crazy to want to be a kicker.

Chapter One

Easton, Pennsylvania

Steve Aponavicius grew up in Easton, Pennsylvania, a town located at the easternmost part of the state where the Delaware and the Lehigh Rivers meet. Not long ago, a newspaper reporter described Easton as a place that was "lost in time." Maybe it's more accurate to say that this town was not so much lost as paused in time, right around the 1980's and early 90's when so many factories and steel plants in the area closed or moved away.

But that's the glass half empty version of the story.

"Lost in time" can also be a compliment to a small town with strong community ties and hard working families, many of them second generation immigrants that have lived there all their lives. It can refer to a place with history and substance; a place that has much more in common with *Leave it to Beaver* than *Keeping up with the Kardashians.*

True, the days of Easton and the entire Lehigh Valley as a major industrial and manufacturing center have passed. The knitting factories of the early twentieth century are long gone. The once mighty Bethlehem Steel Corporation is bankrupt, its Bethlehem plant long closed, its extensive acreage now the home of a cultural arts district which includes the Sands Casino Resort. Even the Wilson, Pennsylvania-based Dixie Cup factory, with its distinctive Dixie Cup water tower, has been sitting empty for years after closing in 1983. Ingersoll Rand is gone. And much of the population is gone, too. Looking for jobs and a different type of future.

Despite this scenario, the incredible fact is that hope exists in Easton. There's a sepia-toned charm about the town, beginning with the Soldier and Sailor's Monument in the middle of downtown's Centre Square and extending down the side streets that are just as likely to have a long established business such as the Easton Café (est. 1946) or the Singer Sewing Machine Shop as the newly opened Intel Wireless store.

Many Americans living in sprawling suburbs or newer, communities comprised mostly of chain stores in strip malls, would be surprised to see a hand-written sign on a family-owned restaurant's front door: *Closed for Vacation.* Not in Easton.

The steel industry and many of the businesses that surrounded or supported it are gone. But Easton still has several points of pride. One involves crayons. The other, involves sports.

When it comes to Easton's famous locals, former world heavyweight boxing champion Larry Holmes, most likely tops the list. In his fighting days, Holmes, who grew up and still lives in Easton, had a killer left jab and was often referred to as "The Easton Assassin."

It's impossible not to think of Holmes while visiting Easton, whether driving along Larry Holmes Drive, grabbing a burger at Larry Holmes Ringside Restaurant, checking out some of the champ's memorabilia at one of his office buildings, L & D Plaza, or working out at Larry Holmes Training Center and Gym. You might even hear his band, Larry Holmes and Marmalade, playing at an event around town.

Easton, or more specifically, the nearby Forks Township, has long been known as the corporate home of Crayola, formerly Binney & Smith, the creators and marketers of one of the most beloved brands in American history, Crayola Crayons. Unlike steel, crayons, markers and colored pencils have remained a constant. In 1996, The Crayola Factory children's museum made its debut in downtown Easton and has been a wildly popular, hands-on tourist destination ever since.

The city of Easton, like much of Pennsylvania, is also famous for football. Namely, high school football of the passionate, Friday Night Lights variety. Over the years, the Keystone State has produced dozens of successful college players and NFL stars, including Johnny Unitas, Joe Namath, Dan Marino, Jim Kelly, Joe Montana and Matt Ryan. And those are just some of the quarterbacks.

In the Lehigh Valley, where several schools (Easton, Liberty, Parkland, and Central Catholic, to name a few) are frequently ranked among the nation's best, there are numerous, longtime rivalries that make high school football the region's main event. Without a doubt, the most heated of these adversarial matchups, named the greatest high school rivalry in the nation by *USA Today* in 2006, is Easton – Phillipsburg.

For over a century, the football teams from Easton High School and Phillipsburg (New Jersey) High School have played each other on Thanksgiving morning. The two schools are from bordering towns, literally divided by the Delaware River, which marks the state line between New Jersey and Pennsylvania.

The game has long been played at Lafayette College, which provides a neutral meeting place and a stadium large enough to accommodate the crowd, which has reached as many as 20,000 fans.

Picture the scene on Thanksgiving morning when throngs of

Phillipsburg residents make their way across the Northhampton Street Bridge into downtown Easton and up the hill to College Avenue. At the same time, most everyone in Easton is making their way to the 10:30 AM game, which despite the holiday, is the highlight of the day.

Due to the early kickoff, many people in both towns rise as early as 5:00 or 6:00 AM to gather their blankets and organized their coolers for the day. Surely the Lehigh Valley area fire departments are on full alert since many people in both towns put their turkeys in the oven to cook while they attend the game.

Over the years, Easton has won the Thanksgiving Day Game fifty-eight times, vs. forty-one for "P-burg". Five games ended in a tie. The contest is played for the Forks of the Delaware Trophy, but mostly, it's all about bragging rights. The winning side will bring up the win constantly during the months following the game; even at a basketball game or soccer game between the two schools.

No question, the win matters to people in these bordering towns. Some families whose team comes out on the losing end don't even bother to make their turkeys that day. For others, whether or not to make and enjoy their meal is a tougher call. Maybe they have a nephew playing for P-burg and a husband who once played for Easton. It's the eastern Pennsylvania version of the Civil War.

The Thanksgiving Day Game has sparked the interest of local as well as national media over the years. In 1988, ESPN televised the game live. Then, in 2004, the network returned to Lafayette College's Fisher Field on Thanksgiving morning to film game highlights to include as part of a series called, *Timeless*. Then, in 2006, ESPN2 broadcast live coverage of the 100th Thanksgiving Day Game played between the two schools. (Easton won, 21-7).

Perhaps most memorably, in April of 2009, ESPN returned to town once more when players from the 1993 Easton and Phillipsburg teams reunited to replay their Thanksgiving Day Game, which ended in a 7-7 tie. The Replay Game, as it became known, grew into a huge event. "Gatorade came in as a sponsor," said Easton High School Head Coach Steve Shiffert. "They had this crazy idea that once you're an athlete, you're an athlete for life. Guys were 120 pounds overweight! They brought in professionals to train them. You can't imagine it. We sold 12,000 tickets in an hour."

For the game, the original coaches from sixteen years prior were brought in, then the sponsors and TV folks provided a little extra help courtesy of assistant coaches Eli Manning (Phillipsburg) and Peyton Manning (Easton) to whip these guys in their mid-thirties into shape.

In the end, the Phillipsburg Stateliners bested the Easton Red Rovers

(27-12), in one of the hottest (it was over one hundred degrees on the field) and toughest (Shiffert said it was one of the most violent he'd seen) games ever to be played between the two rivals.

And so it goes. The tradition continues.

Chapter Two

Easton, by Way of Lithuania

Beginning in the mid-1800's, Easton, like other industry-rich areas of Pennsylvania, was a magnet for immigrants, many of them from Eastern Europe, who came in search of jobs in the coal mines, steel mills and iron foundries. Other waves of immigrants followed, most notably in the early and mid-twentieth century.

After World War II, scores of Eastern Europeans sought to leave their war-ravaged and in some cases, newly Soviet-occupied countries, and make new lives in the United States. Of this group, a significant number who chose the Lehigh Valley of Pennsylvania for their new home were Lithuanians.

The former Soviet Republic of Lithuania is a scrappy little Eastern European country (about half the size of Pennsylvania), which sits on the southeastern shore of the Baltic Sea. Today, Lithuania shares borders with Latvia and Belarus, as well as Poland and the Russian territory of Kaliningrad. But it hasn't always been so.

Ever since the Lithuanian tribes banded together to form a state sometime in the Eleventh Century, the borders of Lithuania have been contracting and expanding. During the Fourteenth Century, the Grand Duchy of Lithuania included present-day Belarus, Ukraine and parts of Poland and Russia, making it the largest country in Europe. Then in 1569, Poland and Lithuania formed the Polish-Lithuanian Commonwealth, which stayed intact for two centuries until the Russian Empire seized most of Lithuania's territory.

After World War I, Lithuania declared its independence and in 1918, once again became a sovereign nation. But its neighbors couldn't seem to resist the strategically important territory and in 1940, not long after the start of World War II, the Soviet Union "annexed" Lithuania. One year later, Nazi Germany attacked the U.S.S.R. and subsequently took over Lithuania. Several years later, as World War II neared an end, the soon-to-be defeated Nazis retreated and the Soviets regained control of Lithuania, which in 1944, became the Lithuanian Soviet Socialist Republic. It would remain so for nearly fifty years.

In the late 1980's, the political and economic reforms of Perestroika and Soviet leader Mikhail Gorbachev's policy of Glasnost (freedom of information and openness in government) led to rumblings of freedom and independence throughout the now former Soviet Union.

But it was tiny Lithuania – David to Russia's Goliath—that became the first Soviet republic to break away from the collapsing USSR. In 1991, Lithuania declared its independence and literally put itself back on the map.

The last Soviet troops left Lithuania in 1993 and by 1994, the reborn Democratic republic was a member of both the European Union and NATO.

Euphemisms such as "annexed" and "occupied" don't begin to do justice to what really happened to the people of Lithuania during the twentieth century. According to *Lithuania: Cultures of the World,* during the Nazi occupation of World War II, some 160,000 Lithuanians were sent to their deaths in concentration camps. When the Soviets re-took the country, some 30,000 resistors were killed and thousands more were deported to Siberian GULAGS. For decades, Catholics, who comprise the majority of Lithuanians, were forced to practice their religion in secret.

More recently, in 1990, the Lithuanian Parliament declared the restoration of independence. The Soviet Union reacted harshly by imposing an economic blockade on its rebellious republic and sending tanks and troops to the capital city of Vilnius. In January of 1991, fourteen civilians were killed when Soviet troops took over radio and TV stations in the city.

Due to a combination of international pressure and enormous political and economic problems on the home front, the Soviets soon accepted Lithuania's resolution of independence and in 1991, the reborn country was admitted into the United Nations.

The story of Lithuania, especially the events surrounding World War II, provides a crucial piece of the Aponavicius family narrative. In 1944, Lithuania was occupied by Nazi Germany, but it soon became clear that the Nazis were going to be forced out by the Soviet army, which would then move in and occupy the country. Although the German occupation was brutal for many Lithuanians, to many, it was actually preferable to Soviet control, which the country had experienced four years prior.

Fearing deportation to Siberian work camps or persecution at home, some eighty-thousand Lithuanians immediately fled the country as the Soviets moved in. Among them were a young married couple, Ben and Filomena Aponavicius, and their six-month old baby boy.

On the day they left their home, which was located halfway between Tverai, where Ben was born, and Aleksandrija, Filomena's childhood home,

Ben Aponavicius, then aged 25, went outside and hitched their horse to a wagon. Then, he and Filomena began loading up as many things as they could carry, mostly essentials such as clothing, food and blankets, as well as a few valuables such as silver and dishes.

They struggled with the last minute decision of what to leave behind, fearing that things such as Filomena's sewing machine might be gone when they returned home. And they had every intention of returning home. Just as soon as the war was over and the Soviets left.

Although the fleeing refugees shared a common goal – to leave until it was safe to return – their chosen destinations varied. Many people went by boat to Sweden, which was neutral during the war and geographically close. Others crossed the border into Poland and stayed there. Many more passed through Poland and continued on to Germany. Others, such as the Aponavicius family, took a coastal route out of Lithuania and directly into Germany.

By the time that Ben, Filomena, and their baby began their journey, the Soviets controlled all but a portion of the country along the Curonian Spit, a peninsula dividing the Baltic Sea from the Curonian (or Courland) Lagoon, into what was then East Prussia (now part of Russia). The sixty or so mile portion of the trip along this mile-wide piece of land was slow and cumbersome as travelers were forced to navigate a series of hills and windswept sand dunes that reached as high as one hundred feet.

At one point, most likely near the town of Nida, the wagon Ben was steering became stuck in some deep sand that had blown onto the dirt road at the bottom of a big hill. The wheels would not budge another inch. So, Filomena and Ben climbed out, unloaded their heaviest things, such as silverware and dishes, and carried them a short distance away from the road. Then, with the intention of returning in a few months to retrieve them, they buried their valuables under a tall tree.

When after several weeks the Aponavicius family finally crossed the border into Germany, their horse was immediately confiscated. (It's possible they were paid for the horse). Then, traveling mostly by train, they made their way to Seubersdorf, a small town where they stayed with a priest and his housekeeper who took them in.

Sometime after the Germans surrendered to the Allies in May of 1945 and World War II was coming to an end, Ben, Filomena, and their now one-year-old son, made their way to Rothenburg, Germany, a Bavarian town that sits high on a plateau overlooking the Tauber River.

They moved into the Wildbad Rothenburg, an impressive, cascading building complex that was built as a spa hotel around the turn of the century, and later became a rehabilitation hospital for German soldiers before it was used to house mostly Lithuanian refugees following the war. (In the early 1980's, the Wildbad became an Evangelical conference center).

Not long after they arrived at the Wildbad, Ben and Filomena's baby boy died of pneumonia. The circumstances and timeline of this heartbreaking event are somewhat hazy because even many years later, Filomena could barely speak about it.

As far as her three other children, Ben, Milda and Ruta, could piece together from what their father and to a lesser degree, their mother, told them, their brother was possibly taken away when they arrived in Rothenburg. According to stories passed down from refugees of this era, many very young children were taken by their German hosts. Although they have no way of verifying this, it's likely that their brother was taken away, and then returned to his parents when he became ill.

Medical supplies were scarce at this time and his condition deteriorated quickly. He died in his mother's arms.

While Ben and Filomena were living in Germany, they had two more children, Ben, Jr., born in 1946, and Milda, born in 1948. Then, in 1949, when more lenient immigration laws were introduced, the Aponavicius family departed for the United States.

Not all the former refugees in Germany left for America. Some stayed where they were and many others went to Canada, Australia or South America. But because Ben and Filomena had made contact with Ben's aunt, Anna Skirutis, who lived in Easton, Pennsylvania, and was willing to sponsor the family, they were permitted to enter the U.S.

Anna Skirutis, whose husband, Joseph, (Ben's uncle) had passed away in 1942, took an enormous leap of faith by sponsoring family members that she had never met. Friends, neighbors and people in her immediate family warned her that she was taking a huge risk accepting responsibility for two people who barely spoke English and their two young children. But Anna never hesitated.

When Ben, Filomena and their children, ages one and three, arrived in New York they took the train to Easton where Anna's daughter met them and drove the family directly to her mother's home.

Although it was not in his field, Ben, who had studied forestry, found work right away. He worked as a dishwasher and busboy at restaurants, mowed lawns and did other odd jobs. After a few weeks with Anna, the family moved into the home of Michael Sungaila, a widower who lived nearby, and soon moved into the bottom floor of a home on Easton's Spruce Street, which no longer stands.

In the summer of 1952, Ben and Filomena purchased a home at 1420 Spruce Street, in part thanks to a loan from Anna Skirutis, which Ben systematically paid back, making his scheduled payment each month. He and

Filomena, who had welcomed another daughter, Ruta, in 1956, lived in the home for the rest of their lives.

It took many years for their children and grandchildren to truly appreciate the obstacles that Ben and Filomena had overcome and the sacrifices they made on their behalf.

In 1993, Kristin Aponavicius Kalbach, one of Ben and Filomena's granddaughters, made a trip to a newly-liberated Lithuania with her father, Ben, Jr., following her college graduation in 1992.

"I think it made me understand my grandparents so much better," Kristin said. "All these quirky things they used to do when I was growing up finally made sense. Oh, that's why my grandma wears a dress and pants at the same time. Everybody in Lithuania does, because it's cold and if you want to wear a dress, you wear both. Or, that's why my grandma sat around peeling potatoes. Everybody in Lithuania peels potatoes. Everybody grows them and peels them while they sit around and talk."

While visiting Lithuania, Ben and Kristin (and a few years later, Ben and his daughter, Lauren, who also made a similar trip), found out many things about their family. According to Ben, he tried to find the location of the valuables that his parents had buried along the road but later learned from them upon his return that he was looking for "the third tree from the fork in the road at the bottom of the hill" on the opposite side of the peninsula that they had crossed.

The family has long given-up the search. The road through Kurisiu Nerija, which is now a national park, has long been paved. Everything has changed. Ben and Filomena have both passed away and although Ben, Jr. still attends Knights of Lithuania meetings and still speaks the language, his children and grandchildren do not.

Even so, the story of where they came from is still a powerful one. Steve Aponavicius and his sisters grew up hearing about the priest who took in their grandparents and a kind woman named Fraulein Minna who helped them in Germany. Ben Aponavicius has faint memories of Rothenburg, and the long, steep steps of the Wildbad and a malicious rooster that his father had to shoo away from him. They try to imagine how it felt to leave your home, not knowing if you would ever be able to return. They think about what it would be like to come to a place where you knew no one and barely spoke the language. They see how they worked and succeeded and made a life their family. And they're grateful. Most of all, they are grateful.

Chapter Three

It's a Boy

In August of 1986, Ben Aponavicius, a chemist, and his wife, Jan, a pre-school teacher, were the parents of two young daughters, Lauren, nearly thirteen years old, and Kristin, who would turn fifteen in one month.

The family lived in a two-and-a-half story white clapboard house with emerald green trim on Coleman Street, in the College Hill section of Easton, Pennsylvania. Like many houses in this tree-lined residential historic district at the top of Easton's bluffs, the Aponavicius home, with its hallmark front gable and covered porch, was built in the early 1900's by the Speer Lumber Company.

Typical of the working class homes in this neighborhood, the house, along with the small, sloping front yard and the fenced-in back yard, was always tidy and well-maintained.

The interior of the house was comfortable and cozy, with three small juxtaposed bedrooms located directly at the top of the staircase on the second floor. The rooms were modest and close together but both Lauren and Kristin had their own bedrooms, a matter of major importance for teenage girls.

Life was good. The girls had friends, school, plenty of activities and their own separate closets. Then, earlier that year, their mother broke the news that the family would soon be expanding.

"I remember when my mother first told us she was having a baby," said Kristin. "My sister and I said, 'I can't believe you just ruined our family. Our family was perfect. Now it's ruined.' We were such selfish teenagers! We were determined to be jerks about it."

Lauren remembers bursting into tears when she heard about the baby. "I was thirteen," she said. "Nothing but attitude. I was not excited."

In her soft, understated way, Jan Aponavicius told her daughters, "Well, this is a done deal. We'll all just have to make the most of it."

When their baby brother, Steven Vitas Aponavicius, was born on August tenth, the girls were away at camp. But when they got home and saw him for the first time, they had an immediate and overwhelming change of heart.

"The minute he was around, we adored him," said Kristin. "It was like he had three moms instead of one mother and two sisters. We totally spoiled him."

The happy, smiling baby with the blonde tuft of hair did his part to charm his sisters but Jan and Ben also helped matters a great deal by enabling the girls to keep their separate bedrooms.

"The girls had never shared a room and we weren't about to throw them together at ages thirteen and fifteen and give this baby his own room," said Jan. "He didn't care where he slept."

So, Baby Steve spent his first year or so sleeping in the closet. Actually, it was a converted walk-in closet that was barely big enough for a crib, a stack of diapers and a few other baby essentials.

He didn't seem to mind, but like most babies, Steve cried occasionally at night and every time he did, Jan immediately went and picked him up.

"I know I spoiled him by never letting him cry," said Jan. "But I didn't want the girls to wake up. We were all right on top of each other!"

By the time he was two years old, Steve had upgraded into a real bedroom. Ben had converted the attic into a fully-finished room, the biggest in the house, which Kristin moved into, freeing up a downstairs bedroom for her brother. When Kristin moved out, Lauren moved upstairs, followed by Steve upon her departure.

Over the years, Steve turned the attic room into the ideal young guy's sports-themed hang-out, complete with a foosball table, several baseball gloves including an outfielder's glove and catcher's mitt, big bags of peanuts from Philadelphia Phillies games and walls covered with Philadelphia Eagles' ticket stubs and team photos from every baseball and soccer team Steve played on from kindergarten through college.

Because Steve's sisters started college when he was very young, (he was three years old when Kristin left for Syracuse University and five years old when Lauren left for the University of Pennsylvania), he effectively grew up as an only child.

Although he established himself as a sports fanatic at a very early age, Steve's first love was trucks. Specifically, garbage trucks.

"We used to keep him home from pre-school on Wednesdays because that was when we had garbage pick-up," said Jan. "He would look out and wait for the trucks to come by."

According to his maternal grandmother, Veronica Damman, Steve would eagerly watch for garbage trucks when she and his grandfather drove him around town.

"He knew every garbage truck on the road," she said.

Even when visiting his grandparents on non-collection days, young Steve still had trash on his mind.

"He used to take my love seat and sofa apart and make recycling bins out of the pillows," said Veronica. "He'd take crumpled up paper and put it in the bins, then he'd take all the stuff to an imaginary drop-off point on the front steps."

Other types of trucks fascinated him, too.

"I remember when they paved our street," said Steve. "That was big! I'd get up early and go outside and watch. I loved it."

According to Jan, when the fire department came to visit Steve's pre-school where she worked, the firemen asked the kids to name the different parts of the truck and from the stabilizers to turret cables, Steve had all the answers.

"A lot of little boys like trucks," said Ben Aponavicius. "But Steve was more fanatical than most."

But the trash trucks were the vehicles that really captured his imagination. When he was four years old, Steve dressed up as a garbage collector on Halloween. When the sanitation workers made their way up Coleman Street that day, the driver and his cohorts on the route stopped and gave him candy. One of the local papers, *The Morning Call,* even ran a picture of Steve and his heroes, who as the paper noted, had painted their faces for Halloween in his honor.

Soon enough, Steve's fixation shifted from trucks to sports. He seemed to make the transition over night and from the time he was five years old, whether he was watching or playing, Steve lived and breathed anything and everything having to do with a ball or a puck.

As a fan, Steve knew every player and every team stat whether he was watching a local high school game or pro football on TV. If he was playing soccer with his friends or hitting baseballs with his dad, there was always time for one more goal kick or one more at bat.

Steve's brother-in-law, Jamie Kalbach, is partly to blame for his obsession. Steve was just three years old when Jamie first met Kristin, when they were both students at Syracuse. Kristin soon brought Jamie home to meet her family and Jamie and Steve were instant friends.
"He was my little buddy at the start," said Jamie. "Whenever I'd go over and visit, we'd start playing, then Jan would have to pull him aside and say, 'Steve, Jamie is here to see Kristin.' He definitely didn't understand that at all."

As far as Kristin was concerned, Jamie earned major points for being so nice to her baby brother.

"I used Steve as a test for my boyfriends," she said. "You could tell the ones that were annoyed and not interested. Then there were the ones who would get on the floor with him. I knew Jamie was a keeper because he was totally involved with Steve. Mom used to have to break them up."

For his part, Jamie, who didn't have a brother of his own, says he was happy to have someone to take to ball games. Jamie and Steve, or sometimes Jamie, Steve, and Kristin, would go to Philadelphia Phillies games, most memorably on Steve's birthday every year when without fail, halfway through the game a crew of well wishers in Phillies garb would come to their seats, sing *Happy Birthday* and throw confetti as Steve's face appeared on the Jumbotron.

Kristin and Jamie, who were in their mid-twenties at the time, still laugh about being mistaken for Steve's parents.

"Wave to Mom and Dad!" people would say to Steve, pointing to Kristin and Jamie, as the Philly Fanatic put his cap on the birthday boy's head.

Jamie also took Steve to Philadelphia Flyers games and later, to Eagles games, but only after he was older and everyone agreed that Steve could handle the raunchy language.

Of course, Jamie and Steve also watched plenty of games on TV. Then, when the game was over, they'd head outside to shoot baskets or throw, kick or hit a ball around. In fact, some members of the family suspect that Jamie may have used Steve as an excuse to cut short his part in family gatherings.

"Sorry to run out," Jamie would shrug, "but the kid wants to go outside and play..."

Jamie and Steve also bonded over their mutual dislike of traditional Lithuanian food that was often served in the Aponavicius home.

"At family meals there was a lot of ethnic food, which I won't eat," said Jamie. "Steve wouldn't eat it either. He was a kid. So we'd get separate meals and that continues to this day. Some of the things they serve are probably great—these lavish potato dishes. But I'd ask for a baked potato and Steve latched onto that. It's my fault."

Besides his brother-in-law, who solidified his allegiance to Philadelphia teams, other family members also influenced Steve, especially went it came to his love of sports. His parents took him to many games at Lafayette College in Easton as well as on bus trips to the Baseball Hall of Fame in Cooperstown or to Baltimore or Boston to see the Phillies play. And Steve's paternal grandfather, Ben Aponavicius, Sr., who Steve called "Pop-Pop", used to take him fishing while visiting Saylorsburg, Pennsylvania, a town on the edge of the Poconos where the family bought a $6000 fixer-upper cabin on Saylor Lake.

Steve and Pop-Pop would row out on to the green water in a rowboat that always seemed to need patching, or they'd cast from the dock just down the hill from the cabin.

"I remember catching these tiny sunfish that weighed something like four ounces," Steve said. "Pop-Pop would spend an hour gutting and cleaning the fish, no matter how small it was so he could cook the fish that I caught. My fish. He was a great, great guy."

Whenever possible, Pop-Pop, who was a forester by trade, spent his time outside.

"Anything outdoors, he loved," said Steve. "Most of my memories are of him working in the garden in our back yard. He planted everything that's back there. Now all those little plants are huge, like a jungle. He even put up a trellis and grew grapes so he and my dad could make wine."

Steve's maternal grandfather, Chris Dammann, (a.k.a. "Pop"), shared Steve's love of baseball, which during his formative years, was his favorite sport.

"My grandfather grew up in Jersey City and played baseball with all these guys who went on to play in the major leagues," said Steve. "He would tell the best stories about playing with this guy or that guy who played with the Yankees. He loved baseball and I'm sure that's a big part of the reason that I came to love it, too. That was our common bond."

Pop also coached Steve's tee ball team when he was seven years old.

"We have the coolest picture hanging up in our house," said Steve. "It's me on my first ever baseball team and my grandfather is standing there, three feet away from me, coaching me up."

Steve's father, Ben, who ran track when he was young and still plays softball in a 65-and-up league, encouraged his son in all his different sports. (He can still beat Steve in tennis). But almost as if he was milking every moment of having a son he didn't expect to have, Ben helped Steve practice and improve his sports skills in a very intense, hands-on kind of way.

"I played sports growing up but I kind of dropped things along the line," said Ben. "Maybe if I'd had someone to encourage me it would have been different. That's why I tried to work so hard with Steve."

Like many dads, Ben would take Steve outside and throw and catch with him. Or, he'd pitch to Steve and patiently retrieve the balls when Steve connected with a hit. But Ben took his fatherly duties to a whole other level. Ben worked as a chemist for Koh-I-Noor, a manufacturer of technical pens and supplies for artists and architects, and true to form, he approached their backyard play in a scientific, formulaic manner, painstakingly breaking down Steve's batting stance and form and even helping his right-handed son become a left-handed batter.

"There's an advantage to hitting left-handed in baseball," said Ben. "I encouraged him very strongly to hit from the left side because you're closer to the base. There are more right-handed pitchers. You hit a ground ball and you can beat it up. From the right side, it's more difficult."

Although Steve batted lefty during most of his baseball playing days and trained himself as a lefty in hockey and soccer as well, he wasn't completely ambidextrous. When he was age five or six, he wore left-handed gloves but couldn't throw left-handed, so he was forced to accept his fate as an officially right-handed player. Nothing wrong with that.

Steve was technically a switch-hitter, a skill he honed while practicing with his dad.

"We'd go over to the tennis courts behind our house and my dad would just pitch to me for hours. I'd hit line drives right at his head! With tennis balls. I refused to hit baseballs at him because I didn't want to kill him.

"Anyway, we went through the entire Phillies line-up, with me taking pitches like the actual players would. It was the '93 Phillies, so, if Lenny Dykstra led off, I would bat left-handed. Then if Mickey Morandini batted second, he was a switch-hitter, so I'd pick which side of the plate I wanted to hit. Then whoever batted third—I think Pete Incabiglia was right-handed-- so I'd switch back over. It was hilarious. But we kept it up for nine full innings."

The analytical, father-son approach to sports extended beyond baseball. Ben, who says Steve was very good with both feet in soccer, gives his son the credit for teaching himself to kick left-footed. But Ben certainly deserves partial credit for helping Steve progress in his post-soccer season hobby of kicking field goals. With a football.

Even though Steve never played organized football during elementary, junior high or high school, he always played pick-up football with his friends. Then, around the time he was eleven or twelve years old, mostly to keep in shape for soccer, he started kicking field goals.

According to Ian McCutcheon, Steve's best friend since they were in second grade, "Steve would go out and kick alone like most guys go out and shoot baskets by themselves."

When he didn't go it alone, Steve would corral Ben and they would head to the middle school a mile or so from their house which had a goal post, but the field was in pretty bad shape. So, ever the problem-solver, Ben got busy and built some uprights in the back yard.

As a base, Ben used the trellis where he and his father formerly grew grapes for their homemade wine. Then, he took two, twenty-foot pieces of wood; flat, skinny, two-by-fours; and nailed them up so they extended vertically from the support poles of the trellis. Bingo! Steve had his uprights.

Although he and Jamie would often go to a park or a school field and kick soccer balls and footballs around just about any time of year, when it came to serious, methodical kicking in the back yard, which had just enough room for an eighteen or twenty-yard attempt, Steve usually stuck to the soccer off-season, which meant the months of November and December.

So, inspired by the NFL play-offs being televised at that time of year, Steve would go outside on cold, Pennsylvania afternoons and kick field goals for hours, once again, studying first, then mimicking the pros.

"The way I learned to kick was by watching David Akers, the Eagles kicker, on TV," Steve said. "He's left-footed, like I was. I'd watch him kick on Sundays and I'd copy exactly what he did.

It was three steps back, three steps over on field goals, which is pretty standard. He took three walking steps then six sort of running steps. That's what I emulated. Even today my field goal steps and my kick-off steps are exactly the same as his. I figured, it worked for him!"

Most of Steve's kicks ended up in the alley behind the back yard, several yards beyond the uprights. But if he kicked it exceptionally hard, or if he shanked it to one side, it would end up in someone else's back yard.

"I think that's where I learned to kick accurately," said Steve. "Because if I missed one way, it would go into this really mean guy's yard. Or, if I missed the other way, it would go into another yard."

If he was alone, Steve would go and retrieve the ball himself. When Ben was with him, he would collect the balls or try to catch them before they hit the ground and toss them back for Steve to kick again.

Soon, they tired of the back yard routine or, more accurately, Steve got to the point where he needed more space. The last straw may have been when a particularly hardy "extra point attempt" toppled one of the posts. In any case, Steve and his volunteer kicking partners moved to the tennis courts for much of their future kicking.

Since the football sailed over the fence on almost every kick, Ben positioned himself on the outside of the tennis court where he stood in the alley, catching balls and throwing them back over the fence. When his hands started to hurt, he sometimes shagged balls by catching them with a trash can, fishing them out and throwing them back.

During an actual football game, another player, known as the holder, takes the snap and positions the ball so the kicker can boot it through the uprights. In practice, kickers often place the ball in a plastic, tripod-like contraption, which is also known as a holder.

At sporting good stores, adjustable kicking holders made of metal cost as much as twenty or thirty dollars, which can become costly given that they're the type of thing that tend to get broken or left behind on a field. So Ben and Steve decided to make their own.

"You can make your own holder for around a dollar," said Steve. "I've probably made ten of them in my life. Me and Dad used to make them all the time. We bought PVC pipe in three-foot increments along with a three-way connector. We even did the math! We used the Pythagorean Theorem to find the height you need to make the holes and stuff. We experimented. If you make it too short, it doesn't work--18 inches is optimal."

So, years before there were YouTube videos on every subject including *How to Make a Field Goal Place Kicking Holder,* Steve and Ben figured it out and had fun doing it. Hardly the caricature of the overbearing father screaming at the refs at his son's game, Ben was the behind-the-scenes guy, who not only stood in a soccer goal for hours as Steve kicked soccer balls at him, but helped him figure out what was working and what was not working.

"He may not have technically known how to coach my kicking," said Steve. "But he could tell me what I did differently each time or what I did with my feet when I kicked a good one."

Mostly, Ben was there for his son. And Jan was, too.

When windows were broken by errant soccer balls, they were tolerant. When they needed to rise at 6:00 AM and drive over an hour for Steve's soccer game, they did it. When Steve played over fifty baseball games in the summer, they came and watched every one. In fact, according to Steve, despite the fact that both his parents were working, he can't recall them ever missing one of his games. Ben and Jan were a constant.

Of course it wasn't all about sports in the Aponavicius home. School and grades were a priority; both Steve's sisters were high academic achievers and he followed in the family mold. Could it be that this straight-A honors student got his homework out of the way (he admits to doing it in front of the TV when the Phillies played) because there was something he would rather be doing?

"He was always a good student," Jan said. "We were lucky. Steve always stayed on top of his homework but it was never his first choice. He'd want to be outside right after school before it got dark. He'd go to practice, then come home and wanted to practice more. He'd always say, 'Just 10 more kicks!'"

When he was in seventh grade, Steve and his best buddy Ian McCutcheon came up with a brilliant plan. They both were sports fanatics and since many of the best contests in Easton were being played right down the street at Lafayette College, they decided to volunteer in the school's sports communications department. That way they could get into all the Lafayette Leopards games for free.

"We got to be around sports, which was what we really wanted to do," Ian said.

Ian's father, Bruce McCutcheon, was the Athletic Director at Lafayette, which gave the boys a definite edge in getting "hired" initially. But they hung in there, never complaining about grunt work or less than glamorous chores. After showing themselves to be ambitious and dependable, Sports Information Director Phil LaBella, and Director of Athletics Communications and Promotions, Scott Morse, kept "promoting" Ian and Steve, giving them more and more responsibilities.

For the most part, Ian and Steve worked at the Leopards football and basketball games, answering phones, calling in score updates, making copies, or serving as spotters (assistants who identify which players make which plays). They also kept statistics, which in the days before computers and the internet, they did by hand.

In the summer, the boys would spend hours updating the school record books by digging around in the university archives to find old football and basketball programs and making notes of which player scored how many points in 1950, 1961 or 1976.

Mostly, Steve and Ian were volunteers, paid only in hotdogs, Cokes and free game tickets. According to Ian's mom, Pat McCutcheon, "They were slave labor, and they loved it."

Occasionally, the two volunteers would land a paying gig especially during basketball tournaments such as the Patriot League championship when ESPN came to town and hired the boys to pull cable and keep stats. Working at those events were thrilling to two young sports fans. But pay was the last thing on their minds.

"We just wanted to do what Phil and Scott were doing," said Steve. "Here we were thirteen and fourteen years old sitting court side at all these basketball games and sitting in the press box at all these football games. And we got to use the weight room. Life was good."

Chapter Four

All About Sports

For Steve, Ian, and most of their friends, the world revolved around sports. When they weren't playing pick-up basketball before soccer practice or working at Lafayette's athletic communications department, they were reading the sports page, arguing about their favorite players, watching games on TV, playing video games or later, covering sports for their high school paper.

During their junior year at Easton Area High School, Steve and Ian, (and other friends including Brandon and Dan Mulrine), wrote for *The Junto,* the school newspaper named for a Philadelphia club started by Ben Franklin in the 1700's. Their chosen topics? Sports, of course.

When they were seniors, Ian took over as editor of the paper, and Steve happily took on the role of sports section editor.

"It was a headache for me because Steve wouldn't show me his stuff until two days before it was due," Ian said. "But then, classic Steve. It would be the best part of the paper!"

Highlights of his days as a sports reporter included a one-on-one interview with Easton High School graduate, Chuck Amato, (Class of 1964), who at the time was the head football coach at North Carolina State. Among other things, Amato and Steve discussed the eleven ACC championships Amato had been a part of: one as a player at NC State (1965), two as an NC State assistant coach (1973 and 1979), and eight at Florida State (1992 through 1999). Of course they also discussed Amato's days as a wrestler and football player at Easton, during the same 1960's era when Steve's dad was a student there.

If they didn't have an organized game or practice to attend, you could find Steve and Ian or Steve's across-the-street neighbor, Pete Karch, playing kickball, street hockey or hitting tennis balls to each other during back yard home run derbies. They'd play knock hockey during pasta dinners the night before soccer games and from time to time, they'd even play quoits, a local game much like horseshoes where players toss a rubber or metal ring called a quoit.

"Growing up, we played every game you can imagine," said Steve. "We even played games we made up. Everything was a competition."

Although Steve loved all sports, if pressed, he would say baseball was his favorite.

"When I think of Steve in an athletic context," said Ian, who played on teams with Steve for many years. "I think of him as a baseball player."

Partly encouraged by his grandfather's love of the sport and his father's participation in what Steve playfully calls, "old man softball," Steve took to baseball right away. When he was just starting out, part of the allure was the uniforms.

"We used to go to the Majestic outlet a few towns over from Easton," said Steve. "They were the manufacturer of major league baseball uniforms and would have huge sales on shirts and caps after a team changed their logos or uniform design, which they did a lot in the early 90's. You could get stuff for a quarter."

During his tee-ball and Little League playing days, Steve stocked up on discontinued togs from every team and proudly wore them to his practices.

"There was a teal Marlins uniform I used to like to wear," he said. "And the matching hat. I was such a punk!"

The second year he played, for a township team called the White Sox, Steve was only called out once the entire season.

"We were coach-pitched back then so every time we got up to bat, the coach would kind of lob it in," said Steve. "I only got out once so my batting average must have been nine hundred and something! They had time limits on the games or they would have gone on forever. We were horrible."

Regardless, Steve's team won the local 10-and-Under championship that season.

"I still remember the Goodyear blimp flying overhead during that game," said Steve. "It was on its way to somewhere else. But it was cool."

Much the same way that he approached kicking in the back yard with his dad, Steve, who mostly played second base, analyzed his baseball skills in a most methodical way.

"He was a student of the game," said Ian. "And he was self-taught. He'd say, 'Hey, I figured out my swing. You put your hands up here like this...'"

Even after his tee-ball and Little League days were done, Steve kept up his analytical approach. According to his high school varsity baseball assistant coach, Greg Hess, "Steve was a very conscientious guy. He was a student on the field; always learning and always inquisitive. I remember once we were going over a play where I wanted him for a cutoff. In the dugout, he said, 'Coach, I gotta ask you why? Why do you want me positioned here?' I'd give him a hard time and say, 'Why do you always have to ask me why? Just do it!'"

Varsity Head Coach Carm La Duca knew that Steve was inquisitive back when he had him as a student in his seventh grade social studies class.

"I knew he was a coach and all I talked about was baseball," said Steve. "At least by the time I got to high school he knew I was interested."

Back in the eighth grade, Steve tried out and started playing for an American Legion team in Easton. This league, founded in 1925 by the revered veteran's service organization, sponsors some 5400 teams in every state in the U.S., plus a few in Puerto Rico and Canada.

American Legion Baseball has deep roots in Pennsylvania; its first World Series was held in Philadelphia in 1926 and Pennsylvania teams have been frequent top contenders over the years.

More than half of current Major League Baseball players competed on Legion teams in junior high and high school before making it in the pros. The list of past MLB stars that played on Legion teams-- everyone from Ted Williams and Yogi Berra to George Brett and Carlton Fisk-- is long and illustrious.

Of all the teams Steve played on growing up, his favorite team name belonged to his Junior Legion team, The Easton Fleas.

"We were named after our sponsor, The Fleas Club," said Steve. "It was a gentlemen's club. Not a strip club, but more of a social club. Although the year we were on the team The Fleas Club got busted by the FBI for this huge illegal gambling ring and got shut down for a while."

Counting their time with the Fleas, Steve and several of his closest friends played Legion ball together for five straight seasons. Despite a less-than-stellar year when they were in the ninth grade in which they finished 1-21, their last three seasons were winners where they won some forty or fifty games. Winning or losing, their camaraderie and love for the game was infectious, especially among their coaches.

"I've been doing this a long time and their class was such a pleasure," said Coach John Bisco. "They were probably the only group of guys that got to practice before I did. If I was in a bad mood, coming from work or whatever, they would immediately put me in a good mood. Besides that, they were really good. So that makes it really fun."

To Steve, the most important thing -- besides winning -- was getting a chance to play.

"We had an all-star second baseman and Steve played second base," said Coach Bisco. "So, when he was a junior I went to him and said, 'What do you want to do?' He said he would do anything to get into the lineup so we worked him at third base and put him in the outfield. He played both just to get his bat in the lineup. He played every game from there on out. You can't do that with the average player but he worked his butt off."

The Legion games, which were played in the summer, directly followed the season for Steve's high school team, which was played in the spring. So, from March until the end of July each year, Steve had a baseball practice or game pretty much every other day.

The grand finale came during Steve's senior year when he played for Easton High School. According to Ian, who played catcher and was the only returning varsity player on the team that year, "We thought we were good but there just weren't a lot of expectations for us to be that good because everyone was so young."

But they were that good. Going into the final week of the season, Easton was a game back from rival Liberty.

"They were always good," said Ian. "They were in the finals every year. They were definitely one of the favorites. We needed a miracle to get into the championship."

Then while Easton won their final game, Liberty lost theirs, which meant the teams were tied. After Easton won their playoff game, it was Liberty vs. Easton in the division championship.

"After we won the playoff, we were celebrating the fact that we were going to the championship game," said Ian. "So, as we were celebrating, our coach put me on the phone with the commissioner of the LVIAC, (The Lehigh Valley Interscholastic Athletic Association), who was flipping a coin to determine who would be the home team. I called tales and we won. Winning that coin toss was probably my greatest contribution to our team."

During the championship game, Easton pulled ahead. Going into the final inning, the Rovers led 6-3, but then, Liberty strung a few hits together, including a ground ball to second base. Steve scooped up the ball and went to tag the Liberty runner, who knocked him to the ground. The umpire called the runner out, but failed to call obstruction, which would have resulted in an automatic Easton double play and the end of the inning. Instead, following the controversial call, Liberty went on to score two runs to tie the game.

Ultimately, the game went nine innings and Easton won with a walk-on base hit. So the final snapshot of Steve's high school baseball career was his team in a celebratory dog pile. The perfect ending.

As much as the spring and summer were about baseball, for Steve, the fall was all about soccer. The first team sport Steve ever played was soccer, when at age six he played for a YMCA team.

In junior high school, Steve played for the Lehigh Valley Magic, a team whose practices were run by the coaches at Lafayette College.

"One of those coaches went to Northwestern and turned their team into a national power," said Steve. "We got to train with a great coach and the core of guys on that team went on to play together in high school. We've got him to thank for all our success."

As a sophomore in high school, Steve played junior varsity soccer on a team that lost only one game. Not only did the team finish 18-1 that year, but the scores were often lopsided with Easton comfortably ahead by halftime of nearly every game.

When Steve made the varsity team his junior year, the first order of business for the varsity boys soccer coach, Tim Hall, who called all his players by their last names, was to learn to say *Aponavicius.*

He pronounced it correctly, which is more than he could say for some of the other guys on the team. One player tried once or twice. Then settled on calling Steve, "Apple Juice."

As a left defensive back, Steve's specialty was kicking the ball hard and deep into the opposing team's territory, a skill that would serve him well in times to come. Ironically, though, the left-footed kicker was almost better known for an often overlooked soccer ability.

"Steve could probably throw in the ball thirty yards or more," said teammate Andy Hill. "He could kick the ball further than just about anyone else. But the throws? He did his job with those."

According to his coach, Steve would deflect any compliments about his throws.

"He was humble about it," said Hall. "He'd say things like, 'So and so are the good ones. I just throw in the ball for them.'"

That year, Steve was named a Scholar Athlete Nominee by both the conference and the Lehigh Valley Soccer Coaches Association. He also won Honorable Mention All-Division and All-Area, which according to Coach Hall, is rare for a defender.

"He was a defensive guy," said Coach Hall. "He probably could have played forward but we had enough forwards. That's just how Steve was. He'd play wherever we could use him. And he did great in the back."

Steve did get one shot at forward, though. In fact, he literally got two shots, when during Easton's senior night game, with the team up by several goals, the forwards and the defenders switched positions at the end of the game. In just five minutes, Steve scored two goals.

Fittingly, the most memorable game of Steve's soccer career was the final regular season match of his senior year, when Easton beat heavily favored Emmaus to win the 2004 Lehigh Valley Conference Championship. Emmaus, which came into the game ranked ninth in the entire Northeast, had beaten Easton earlier in the season. They also were the team responsible for the only loss by Steve's JV squad two years prior.

According to Steve, the championship was played on a cold, misty evening in front of a less than capacity crowd of five hundred. By the second half, the mist turned into a driving rain, which no doubt shrunk the crowd even more.

With just five minutes to go, the game remained scoreless. Players on both sides were anticipating overtime, but then Steve's teammate, Andrew Goldstein, connected with a rolling ball and scored from some thirty-five yards away.

The victory marked the first soccer championship in the history of Easton High School's then forty-year program. For the players, celebrating and dumping the remains of the water cooler on their already soaking wet coach, then being presented with their medals and championship trophy were sweet moments. But sweeter still was being congratulated by everyone in school the next day. In a place where football is king, a soccer player could get used to that.

It's not unusual for high school soccer players to also kick for their football teams. In fact, many football coaches across the country actively recruit soccer players for kickoff, extra point and field goal duties.

Over the years, the highly successful Easton Red Rovers football team (#2 in all time wins in Pennsylvania and #10 in all time wins nationwide), have had their share of kickers on their roster that used to play or currently played soccer. But Steve Aponavicius wasn't one of them.

One reason, according to Steve, was that the team already had several very good kickers. Another reason, he was busy with soccer in the fall.

No matter what sport you play or don't play, high school football is an enormous part of everyone's life in Easton, Pennsylvania. It can't be avoided. It's the fervent talk of the town all year long and few Easton residents, and virtually no Easton High School students, would dream of missing a Friday night football game.

Steve never missed a Red Rovers football game from the time he was in the fifth grade. When he got to high school, he was fired up to be a fully invested fan sitting in the student section. Then, during his sophomore year, Steve and some of his friends turned being a spectator into a sport all its own when they started something called Rover Nation.

To accommodate the large crowds, Easton High School home football games are played at Cottingham Stadium in downtown Easton, with the exception of the annual Thanksgiving game against Phillipsburg High School, which is played at Lafayette College's Fisher Field.

At the time, the tradition at Cottingham was that juniors and seniors sat in their own section on the fifty-yard line, while freshman and sophomores sat in another section down near one of the end zones.

Inevitably, competitions sprang up between sections with classes trying to outdo each other by showing the most spirit and making the most noise.

The seniors had advantages such as experience, superior real estate and the backing of the band, which sat directly behind them. Even so, the sophomores of the Class of 2005, who at one point, covertly moved right next to the seniors and showed them up, soon proved to be top dogs when it came to cheering on the Red Rovers.

According to Ian McCutcheon, things evolved organically.

"It was towards the beginning of this one game," Ian said. "Things were kind of dead. People weren't into it. So, someone said, 'We need some atmosphere here!' So we took off our shirts and one of the girls had some lipstick so we could put letters on our chests. It was very makeshift at first, but it was a blast. We thought, we need to make a habit of this. The next week we got organized."

Hence, Rover Nation, originally referred to as The Super Sophomores, was born. At first, give or take ten guys (no girls were official members until a few years later), the core group included Ian, Steve, Brandon and Danny Mulrine, Ryan Kavscak, Cory Golden, Pete Cheng, Alex Krom, Steve Martucci and Mark Chando, who Steve credits as the first guy to take his shirt off at a game.

Soon enough, the entire group would gain fame for painting their faces and bodies, with each one "wearing" a letter on his bare chest so when they stood together in the stands it would spell out E-A-S-T-O-N or if they had enough people, E-A-S-T-O-N R-O-V-E-R-S ! or as they gained more participants, G-O E-A-S-T-O-N R-O-V-E-R-S !!! Steve's paint job, which included a three-dimensional bra, was especially inspired.

The friends would always get together each week a day or two prior to the games to make plans, draw signs, buy body paint, and most importantly, organize their props and wardrobe.

Because they went shirtless to the games, the members of Rover Nation didn't need shirts. But they did need pants, (Steve wore vintage Easton High School football pants), shoes, and most importantly, headwear.

Ian wore a lampshade. Steve wore an old fedora that he painted in school colors (red and black). Others wore everything from a fireman's helmet and fencing mask to a scuba mask and snorkel.

Basically, it depended on what they could scrounge together.

"It was whatever we could find in our garages," said Brandon Mulrine, who painted the letter "A" on his bare chest each week. "We also did our fair share of dumpster diving."

Once, the guys stumbled upon a gold mine when Brandon's dad, Mark Mulrine, tipped them off that a local shopping center was going out of business and the dumpster behind the store was a treasure trove of props.

"A pet store and a beer store had moved and left all this great stuff," said Steve. "We got maybe a hundred rawhide bones which was perfect. Our mascot is a bulldog, a red rover, so the whole student cheering section had dog bones. We also got cardboard cutouts of the St. Pauli Girl and a NASCAR driver. We painted over the beer logos with, 'Go Easton!' We were literally crawling around in this dumpster. That's the kind of dedication we had."

Of course their dedication, which became well known throughout the Lehigh Valley, extended to game day.

"Our stadium is a cozy little place," said longtime Easton head football coach, Steve Shiffert.

"The pre-game is pretty interesting because the opponents have to warm-up right in front of the Rover Nation. These kids came early to give the visitors the works during warm-ups. People don't like to come here and play because the Rover Nation and the band make it such a loud place. It's a little bit of a hostile environment."

The Nation also took their show on the road for away games, displaying just as much, if not more, exuberance than they did at home.

"During our sophomore year we were playing Freedom at the stadium they shared with Liberty in Bethlehem," said Ian. "Some Freedom kids were walking around the track and some Easton kids yelled something, then they yelled back. Anyway, these police officers came over to us and said, 'Everyone has to go.' We said, 'Really?' I mean, we'd had no part of it. They ended up clearing out the entire student section. We stood outside to watch the rest of the game."

Evidently, when the cops are looking for a suspect, the painted-up guy with the sombrero stands out. But Steve, Ian and their gang put a creative spin on the incident. The following week, they added homemade, tinfoil halos to their headgear.

People were always asking the members of Rover Nation how they could stand to be shirtless during the cold, sometimes sub zero, Pennsylvania fall and winter.

"Temperature is a state of mind," said Ian.

"We wore gloves," said Brandon "And headwear."

Although Jean Mulrine worried that her son, Danny, once exhibited signs of hypothermia, according to Pat McCutcheon, her son, Ian, never got sick.

"I'd hear that other parents were asking, 'Does Mrs. McCutcheon know the boys aren't wearing shirts?" she laughed. "I'd say, we know where they are and what they're doing and we think it's great. They're not out smoking pot in the parking lot. It was good, clean, fun."

Jan Aponavicius agreed.

"They were so focused on supporting their team," she said. "There was nothing to hate about it except for the fact that our shower was black and red all the time."

"And the paint on the upholstery in our cars," added Ben Aponavcius. "I think they still have paint on them."

Washing off the paint was definitely an issue.

"Some nights I'd come home too tired to scrub off the paint so I'd put on two shirts to sleep in, then I'd take a shower in the morning," said Steve. "It was really hard to get it off the body. The red and black would turn orange in our tub. It was so gross! It took a long time to get clean. I'd still have the outline of a 'T' on my chest and it wouldn't fully come off until Tuesday or Wednesday of the next week."

To keep their momentum going between games, the Rover Nation guys had t-shirts made up with a logo designed by Rover Nation artist, Dan Fuher and wore them to school. They even started selling them to other students, although the school administration pulled the plug on one particular version.

"One of our huge rivals is the Parkland Trojans," said Brandon. "Ian came up with the idea to make t-shirts with the Trojan helmet with a red slash through it on the front and on the back we put the slogan, 'Trojans are only good once.' We put that because they won the conference title the year before. Anyway, we had to stop selling those. I guess they were deemed inappropriate for school wear."

The Rover Nation, which had swelled to include a large percentage of the student body, got plenty of recognition around Easton. The local papers ran pictures of the group at games and one year, they were invited on The Big Ticket, a local Friday night high school football TV show.

"It was right before Halloween, so we carved our logo and The Big Ticket logo into pumpkins and put them on a stand," said Brandon. "My mom's a chef, so we got a big soup cauldron and put dry ice and a smoky thing in there. We crammed about fifty of us in the studio, all yelling and screaming in the background. It was awesome."

Although the last direct links to the founding members graduated with Ian's younger brother, Gavin, in 2011, Rover Nation is thriving and still known as one of the most enthusiastic and intimidating cheering sections in high school sports. One thing is different, though. These days, all the Easton High School students sit in one section during games, a change that came about when the founders approached the school administration during their senior year and offered to forgo their exclusive rights to fifty-yard line seats in exchange for a more unified, inclusive, all class student section.

All for one and one for all when it comes to being as loud as possible. Especially during the annual Thanksgiving Day Game between Easton and

Phillipsburg. For seniors at Easton High School, the game and the week leading up to it is the highlight of the year. Besides the game, the focal point of Easton-P-burg week is the traditional Wednesday night bonfire and pep rally.

To build a bonfire worthy of the Thursday game, members of the senior class start collecting wood on Tuesday. They fan out around town hitting up local residents and businesses for old wooden pallets, broken chairs, or any discarded plywood or lumber of any kind. A falling down wood shed or planks from a dismantled deck? Jackpot.

Local business owners also help out, sending truckloads of wood and other tinder to the bonfire site for the seniors to unload and stack onto the rising pile. As the structure for the bonfire is being assembled, it is constantly attended. In fact, the seniors, who don't have classes that week, camp out on Tuesday night, sleeping in tents and sleeping bags while taking turns keeping watch.

"The legend goes that some time in the 1960's, P-burg had come and lit the bonfire the night before," said Ian McCutcheon. "I'm not sure if that's an urban legend or not, but the tradition is to sleep out and protect our wood."

It's likely that the P-burg residents are jealous of the Easton bonfire. New Jersey law prohibits them from having one of their own. They have to make do with fireworks.

In any case, the Class of 2005 kept the Tuesday tradition alive. When the bulk of the work was done for the day, the seniors pitched tents and set up grills for cooking out. They dressed in layers and drank hot chocolate to fight off the cold. They played games. Some of them never slept. According to his friend, Ian, Steve was not among the sleepless.

"Steve and Brandon actually did go to sleep because they felt they needed to be prepared and rested for the next day. 'I said, 'Really? You can't go on adrenaline?' I guess Steve's priorities were straight. He thought wood-collecting and being ready for the game were so important."

Indeed, there was more work to be done Wednesday morning, when the seniors finished arranging the bonfire. Then, before the parade from the old to the new high school and the pep rally that night, the founding members of Rover Nation painted-up and got into full costume, a gesture that was both noticed and appreciated by the football players.

"I remember one of the captains giving a speech and saying, 'We really appreciate kids wearing lampshades and drawing bras on themselves to cheer us on every Friday. You want to be an Easton football player because of fans like these.'"

The night before the game, as they did prior to every Thanksgiving Day Game, Steve and fifteen friends spent the night at the Aponavicius home, which is just a couple of blocks from Lafayette's stadium.

"We'd sleep anywhere and everywhere, all over the floor," said Steve. "Then we'd wake up at seven or eight o'clock and head to the game and start yelling at the other team during their warm-up. It was a way of life for us."

Of course, the game was the big draw. That year, both teams entered the game undefeated for only the second time in the history of the rivalry that began in 1894, which was twelve years before the legalization of the forward pass. Thanks to several bad punt snaps from Phillipsburg's long snapper, a pre-game heckling target of the Rover Nation, the standing-room-only crowd of over 15,000 watched Easton jump out to an early lead they would never relinquish. The Rovers dominated every facet of the game, winning 31-0.

For Steve and his friends, you'd be hard-pressed to find a more exhilarating and satisfying day.

Kindergarten-bound.

Watching sports on TV with Dad.

Aspiring Garbage Men
(L to R): Anthony Kriel,
Ben Chartier-Cotter,
Steve and Pete Karch

Pop Dammann
and Steve.
June 1990

(L to R):
Steve and brother-in-
law Jamie after the
Phillies lost.
July 1993

(L to R): Kristin,
Steve and Lauren on
Lauren's wedding day
2000

Steve and Pete Karch.
Going through the
Phillies line-up.

The original Rover Nation. "Temperature is a state of mind."

Steve Aponavicius, the walk-on.

Built-in fan base: Kristin, Jamie and Steve's nephews Tyler and Bradley.

For some reason, Grandma Dammann loves BC football.

The name almost
didn't fit.

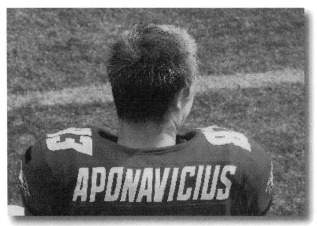

Jan and Ben made it to almost
every one of Steve's games,
home and away.

Be Smooth.

Chapter Five

Boston College

In June of 2005, Steve graduated with honors near the top of his high school class, twelfth out of nearly seven hundred students. With his grade point average, class rank, high SAT scores and myriad of extracurricular activities and honors including membership in the National Honor Society and Who's Who Among American High School Students, Steve had many options when it came to choosing a college. His father, Ben, graduated from Lafayette College in Easton but Steve was ready to venture farther from home. His sister, Kristin, went to Syracuse and his sister, Lauren, went to The University of Pennsylvania for undergrad, then to the University of Michigan for graduate school.

Inspired by Lauren and her husband, Brian, Steve planned to study business and considered several top schools. As he narrowed the field, his final choices came down to Maryland,(where he'd been accepted into the honors program), Michigan, Penn State and Boston College.

For a number of reasons (his Mom loved the small, Catholic college; it was closer to home than Michigan; business students are enrolled in the business school right away; etc.), Steve was leaning towards the prestigious and highly selective Boston College. Then, when BC ultimately offered the best financial aid package, his decision was made.

Located in the serene-by-Boston-standards suburb of Chestnut Hill, geographically, BC keeps some incredibly impressive company. Just across the Charles River and a few miles down the road in either direction you'll find some of the top schools in the country including Harvard, M.I.T., and Northeastern. There are fifty-plus colleges and universities in the greater Boston area, and some, such as Boston University, boast huge enrollments of more than 30,000 students.

With its quiet, almost pastoral campus and relatively small student body of 9,100 undergraduate and 4,500 graduate students, it would have been understandable if Boston College developed an inferiority complex over the years. Instead, BC has become one of the most selective and top-ranked universities in the country, consistently excelling in every category from academics to athletics.

According to *U.S. News & World Report,* Boston College is ranked fifth among the top-ten most applied-to private institutions in the country and in 2010 was ranked thirty-first overall among the nation's universities. Forbes.com ranked BC sixteenth in its 2009 edition of *America's Best Colleges.*

From the nearly 30,000 applications in 2009, the acceptance rate was a highly selective thirty-one percent. Over eighty percent of students in the most recent incoming freshman class averaged 2004 on their SAT's and were in the top ten percent of their high school class.

Yes, the campus and student body are small. But the caliber of students, alumni and faculty, which hail from all fifty states and eighty countries, are of the highest quality. You might say that pound-for-pound, BC is one of the best universities in the U.S.

To better understand what Boston College is and how it evolved, it's best to start at the beginning. Boston College was established in 1863 by the Society of Jesus (the Jesuits), an order of religious men originally founded in Paris in the mid-sixteenth century by seven idealistic students who wanted to serve the needs of the Catholic Church and their fellow men and women.

By the mid-1800's, the Jesuits were becoming synonymous with their approach to quality education that included equal parts intellectual excellence, religious commitment and service. From the start, Jesuit institutions sought to develop a student's character as well as his intellect. Boston College began with those ideals in mind; the goal was to establish a liberal arts institution with emphasis on Greek and Latin classics, English and modern languages, philosophy and religion.

As heady as that sounds, BC's inaugural years were actually quite humble. The first classes which took place on September 5, 1864, were taught by three instructors to a total of twenty-two students who ranged in age from eleven to sixteen. (Initially, BC offered a seven-year high school through college program).

There had actually been several attempts to establish a Jesuit school in Boston prior to BC's official opening. In 1827, Benedict Joseph Fenwick, S.J., the second Bishop of Boston, opened a short-lived school in the basement of his church, The Cathedral of the Holy Cross, but failed to attract other Jesuit teachers and administrators. Fenwick finally secured a faculty in 1843, but feeling resistance from Boston's protestant leaders, he elected to open the school (which became the College of the Holy Cross) outside of Boston in Worcester, Massachusetts.

Then a few years later, John McElroy, S.J., a Jesuit priest from Maryland was transferred to Boston and set about raising funds for a Jesuit high school and college primarily to serve the growing Irish Catholic immigrant population.

In 1857, McElroy purchased land on Harrison Avenue in Boston's South End where Boston College in its earliest incarnation would be built.

The school, which initially consisted of a schoolhouse and a church, opened in 1859 but faced insurmountable problems, not the least of which was the beginning of the nation's bloody Civil War. Further, due largely to the anti-Catholic bias still prevalent in this era, Boston College failed to obtain a university charter from the Massachusetts legislature and just two years after opening, was forced to close its doors. Then, in 1863, the charter was granted and the following year classes once again commenced at Boston College and Boston College High School.

During the first decade or so of operations, BC expanded onto James Street and over the years an effort was made to separate the high school from the college buildings, which at first shared quarters. But by the turn of the century, BC's enrollment had expanded to five hundred-plus and the alumni and faculty realized the college had outgrown its urban setting.

In 1907, BC's new president, Thomas I. Gasson, S.J., purchased Amos Adams Lawrence's farm in rural Chestnut Hill, some six miles west of the city, and the college officially moved to its new and present location.

In June 1909, ground was broken for construction of the new campus, which architect Charles Donagh Maginnis originally envisioned as twenty English Collegiate Gothic style buildings with the working title of Oxford in America.

Despite the grand intentions, progress was slow. The first building, Gasson Hall, known at the time as the Recitation Building, didn't open until four years later in March 1913, and would remain BC's only new building for several years until funds for additional construction could be raised. In the mean time, faculty and students utilized buildings from the former farm including a barn and a gatehouse.

The original, highly ambitious Oxford in America plan was scaled down somewhat and over the next decade or so, three more buildings were added to the skyline of the campus now known as The Heights: St. Mary's Hall (1917), Devlin Hall (1924), and Bapst Library (1928).

As the campus filled out, so did the components of BC's university charter. During the roaring '20's, a Summer Session was added and the Graduate School of Arts and Sciences, the Boston College Law School, the Woods College of Advancing Studies and the Evening College all opened for business. In the 1930's, the BC Graduate School of Social Work and the College of Business Administration, (now known as the Carroll School of Management) began operations.

Physically, BC continued its steady growth. In the 1940's, new land and building acquisitions doubled the size of the main campus and by 1947, BC had a School of Nursing and soon after, in 1952, a School of Education.

Also in 1952, The Graduate School of Arts and Sciences offered its first doctoral programs and soon, the graduate schools of Education, Nursing, Management and Social Work followed suit.

In 1974, BC purchased the nearby Newton College of the Sacred Heart and folded its forty acres and fifteen buildings into its campus. (Today this is the site of the Law School and residence halls housing more than eight hundred students). To further add to its geographical layout, in 2004 the university acquired forty-three acres from the Archdiocese of Boston, a piece of land adjacent to the now 175-acre main campus now referred to as the Brighton Campus.

Other properties which today are also officially part of the campus include the twenty-acre seismology research observatory and field station in Weston, Massachusetts; an eighty-acre retreat center in Dover, Massachusetts; and the Centre for Irish Programmes: Dublin, on St. Stephen's Green in Dublin, Ireland.

Over the years, fund-raising initiatives have continued to enhance not only the physical campus, but the resources of the university itself. Back in 1997, then new-President William P. Leahy, S.J., continued the efforts begun by his predecessor, J. Donald Monan, S.J., when he announced the plan for "Advancing the Legacy," BC's $260 million, five-year investment to strengthen education, reaffirm its Jesuit and Catholic mission, increase research, and improve the quality of student life.

Two years later, the university followed with a $400 million fund raising campaign, "Ever to Excel: The Campaign for Boston College," which set the goals of adding one-hundred endowed university chairs, fifty million dollars worth of undergraduate and graduate financial aid, as well as targeting support for academic centers, libraries, and selected undergraduate and graduate programs, and helping to fund new construction, including a planned student center and humanities building.

Meanwhile, Boston College is still evolving, as evidenced by other initiatives, including "Light the World," the 2008 fundraising campaign which set the goal of raising a lofty 1.5 billion as part of the school's 150th anniversary celebration in 2013, and "The Master Plan", a $1.6 billion, ten-year plan to revamp the campus and hire new faculty, which is underway after being approved by Boston's mayor and zoning commission in 2009.

With over 155,000 alumni, BC boasts the largest Catholic alumni association in the world. One of Boston College's early grads (Class of 1885), was John F. "Honey Fitz" Fitzgerald, the first Irish Catholic Mayor of Boston and the grandfather of future U.S. President John F. Kennedy.

Other notable grads over the years include John Kerry, the U.S. Senator from Massachusetts and 2004 Democratic Presidential nominee; the late Tip O'Neill, speaker of the U.S. House of Representatives; Paul Cellucci, the former Governor of Massachusetts and U.S. Ambassador to Canada; and the late Richard Cushing, American Cardinal of the Roman Catholic Church.

The long and impressive list of BC graduates in the world of business includes G. Craig Sullivan, former Chairman and CEO of Clorox, Co.; Robert Leonard, President and CEO of Ticketmaster; and Aleksandar Totic, co-founder of Netscape; just to name a few. Sports columnist, Mike Lupica; *McLaughlin Group* host, John McLaughlin; and co-host of *The View,* Elisabeth Hasselbeck; all graduated from The Heights, as did *Saturday Night Live* cast member turned movie star, Amy Poehler.

BC has also sent its share of star grads into the sports world, including Heisman Trophy winner Doug Flutie and current NFL stars Matt Ryan and Matt Hasselbeck (brother-in-law of Elisabeth Hasselbeck).

Over the years, Boston College has developed a reputation as a top-notch sports school not only for the impressive winning records of its teams, but also for the high level academic performance of its student athletes.

According to 2009 NCAA statistics, BC's Graduation Success Rate (GSR) was ninety-six percent for all student athletes, which means it ranks among the top nine in the country for Division I schools. (The average GSR nationwide was seventy-eight percent). Regarding football players, BC tied with Duke for the fourth best GSR (92) in the country, following third place Stanford (93), second place Notre Dame (94), and first place Navy (95). In previous years, BC has won the American Football Coaches Association's Academic Achievement Award four times and received Honorable Mention fifteen times.

As notable as the football team's recent numbers are, the GSR has been even higher in the past. In 2006, it was ninety-six percent and in 2004, The Boston College Eagles graduated one hundred percent of the senior players!

Today, the football team competes in Division I of the National Collegiate Athletic Association (NCAA) as members of the Atlantic Coast Conference (ACC). Other teams at BC compete in the ACC as well, if the sport is offered within the conference.

Men's sports include baseball, basketball, cross country, fencing, football, golf, ice hockey, sailing, skiing, soccer, swimming, tennis, and track & field. Women's sports include basketball, cross country, fencing, field hockey, golf, ice hockey, lacrosse, rowing, sailing, skiing, soccer, softball, swimming, tennis, track & field, and volleyball.

In terms of national and on-campus attention, Eagles football gets the most buzz. But it's not unusual for hockey to take center stage at BC. The men's hockey team has won the NCAA National Championship twice (in 2001 and 2008) in the last ten years.

Hockey is also at the center of one of the most exciting traditions at BC, the Beanpot Championship, an annual men's hockey tournament played at TD Banknorth Garden in downtown Boston between teams from Boston College, Boston University, Northeastern and Harvard. A similar tournament is also played between the school's baseball teams, but the hockey tournament, which was first played in December of 1952, is the big draw.

The first Beanpot was played in the Boston (now Matthews) Arena during its first staging, then the tournament was moved to the Boston (now TD Banknorth) Garden. Early on, games were played in December and January, mostly to fill the arena, which didn't have many events scheduled that time of year.

Then, during the sixth year of the tournament, the current "first two Mondays in February" format was adopted. (Note: the women's tournament, which began in 1979, is played on the first two Tuesdays of February at the Bright Hockey Center in Cambridge, Massachusetts).

The tournament, which has been selling out all 13,909 seats ever since the early 1960's remains one of the hottest tickets in town. Boston College has won the men's tournament 14 times and the women have brought home the trophy four times (three times since 2006). For Eagles fans, one of the most anticipated pre-game activities is gathering outside of the BC T-stop (public transportation stop) before the BC-BU games and trying to pack as many cars as possible, thus preventing BU fans from boarding and beating them to the game. Good, cold fun.

All BC teams and Superfans wear the school colors, maroon and gold. They also share the school mascot, The Eagle, or Baldwin, as the game-day representation of the BC Eagle is known today. Back in BC's early days, the school didn't even have an official mascot. Then, in the spring of 1920, the track team won the Eastern Intercollegiate competition and a cartoonist, Charlie Donelan of the *Boston Traveler* newspaper, depicted BC as a stray cat lapping up the competition.

BC fans didn't appreciate the depiction and one alumnus in particular, Rev. Edward J. McLaughlin, argued that the mangy cat cartoon would not have appeared if BC had a proper mascot, so he put his protest in writing and sent it to the school newspaper, *The Heights*.

"Why not select the eagle, symbolic of majesty, power, and freedom," wrote McLaughlin. "Its natural habitat is the high places. Surely, the Heights is made to order for such a suggestion."

A special edition of *The Heights* published early that summer featured a drawing of the new eagle mascot soaring above the school banner. The eagle it was, but Baldwin in his current form (so named for *bald,* as in *eagle,* and *win* as in *win*), didn't appear for a few decades.

BC's first live mascot was a majestic bird (actually, it was a hawk), which was presented to the school as a gift in 1923. The bird had a great back story – it survived a horrific storm and landed on a fishing schooner whose crew rescued it after it became caught in the ship's rigging.

The next year, BC received an actual eagle but it was soon transferred to a zoo when its conditions on campus became too taxing.

For the next forty years or so, BC's mascot was a stuffed, mounted golden eagle named Herpy. Then, in 1961, another live eagle named Margo for maroon *(Mar)* and gold *(go),* was put to work firing up the fans. After Margo died in 1966, the six-and-a-half-foot Baldwin character was born. The nine-and-a-half-foot Baldwin, Jr., came later, and today, both Baldwin and Baldwin, Jr. are fixtures at Boston College sporting events.

Sports are an important part of college life at BC and the school's strong sports program played a significant role in Steve's choice to become a student there.

"I wanted to be at a school with really good teams," said Steve. "It's part of the reason I picked the place. The basketball team was really good— they won a Big East Championship in 2001—and the football program was in the top 25."

Mostly, Steve's interest in BC sports was from the perspective of a fan or a spectator. Beyond participating in intramurals or pick-up games, as far as he knew when he headed off to school, he would not be playing on a university team. This was definitely a disappointment to Steve.

"I wanted to play baseball at BC," said Steve. "So, back in the summer I e-mailed the baseball coach and he basically told me they didn't accept walk-ons. Most teams don't. There are only twenty-five guys on the team so they don't need practice bodies like you do in football. So, to play, you have to have been recruited."

Not playing on a team was a letdown as well as an enormous change for an eighteen-year-old who had played some sort of sport or had a practice to attend almost every day of his life as far back as he could remember. Even though his classes were sure to be demanding, Steve wondered what he would do during his down time.

Instead of feeling sorry for himself, Steve decided to get busy. After all, Boston College had a football team—a pretty good one—and surely there were fans like him who took fandom seriously.

So, before leaving for Chestnut Hill in August, Steve gathered several fireman's helmets and a safari hat he'd found while rummaging around a flea market with his dad. Next, he took to the back yard to paint them bright yellow (gold), the same color as the Superfan t-shirts that BC students wore in the stands. Then, he finished them off by tracing the BC logo on the front of each hat. He went shopping for body paint in BC's school colors and even asked Danny's dad, Sean Mulrine, to be on the lookout for some gold football pants that he could wear as part of his new game getup.

True, his Rover Nation buddies wouldn't be with him. Brandon Mulrine was en route to the United States Military Academy, Dan Mulrine would be going to South Carolina, and Ian McCutcheon was starting at Lafayette College in the fall. Even so, Steve was sure that he would find like-minded friends who would support the Boston College Eagles in a manner befitting a true fan.

So Steve loaded the car with his Superfan supplies, along with some clothes, dorm room staples, and a duffle bag packed with a few footballs and his homemade kicking holders, (old habits die hard), and headed to Boston.

A day or two before classes started, Steve was hanging out in his dorm room without anything much to do. He'd met his roommates and a couple of guys on his hall, but he really didn't know anybody yet. He didn't feel like playing a video game or calling a friend back home or watching TV. He was restless and definitely felt like getting out of the tiny room, a "forced triple" where three freshman share a room originally intended for two.

So, Steve dug into his duffel bag, grabbed a football and a holder-- one of the PVC pipe contraptions he built with his dad-- and headed out to find a field or somewhere he could make some kicks.

As he began walking the long downhill route from upper to lower campus, he decided to keep on going and head all the way to Alumni Stadium. He was excited to see what the building was like inside, so he approached the gate to have a look. To his surprise, the stadium was open. Unlocked. There were maybe five or six people inside, sitting on the bleachers reading or jogging around the track.

So Steve walked through the gate and out to the middle of the field, put the holder down, set the football on it, walked a few steps back, approached the ball and kicked it through the uprights. Then, he jogged into the end zone, picked up the ball and jogged back out to the middle of the field, set up and kicked it again.

The next day, school was officially in session. Steve went to his classes, Exploring Catholicism and Computers and Management, then went back to his dorm and flopped down on his bed. Once again, boredom set in. It was late afternoon, there was plenty of daylight left, so Steve grabbed his holder and football and headed to the stadium.

Once again, the stadium was unlocked and as far as he could tell, this time, it was completely empty. It was strange to be alone in that enormous place. As he walked through the open gate and down the ramp onto the turf, Steve found himself walking softly like a prowler and looking back several times to see if anyone was watching him. The coast was clear so he kept walking towards the middle of the field.

When he reached the forty-yard line, Steve knelt down, set up his holder, and put the football in place, leaning it at a slight angle. As he stood up and walked back a few yards, he looked around at the 40,000 empty seats surrounding him, trying to imagine what the place would look like with a packed, cheering crowd. He looked up at the lights and the lettering across the upper deck, *Alumni Stadium – Home of the Eagles* and couldn't help but grin.

"This is going to be great," he thought. In just a few days, he would be here in this stadium watching his first live BC football game with all the other Superfans. The Eagles had already played one game—an away game against BYU the previous weekend. But in a few days, they'd be returning home and Steve could hardly wait.

Getting back to business, he took three long strides and kicked the ball through the uprights. He jogged over to the end zone, picked up the ball and did it all again.

Steve had been kicking for about a half an hour when out of the corner of his eye, he noticed a guy walking down the sideline at a fast clip. Steve was about to kick the ball again when he turned and saw that the guy had stopped and was standing there watching him.

Steve stood there for a minute, looking at the guy looking in his direction. Then the guy started walking towards him. Thinking he was about to be booted off the field, Steve picked up the ball and holder, and waved to the guy, acknowledging that he'd seen him and was about to leave.

"So, you kick?" said the guy, who introduced himself as assistant football coach Jay Civetti. "We just had a kicker quit during camp. We could use another kicker to help us out…"

Steve could not believe what he was hearing. Not only was the guy not kicking him off the field, but he was asking him if he was interested in kicking for the Boston College Eagles.

"I didn't kick in high school or anything," Steve stammered. Then, in a moment of clarity, Steve realized that it mattered what he said next. It was like an "elevator moment" where an employee gets thirty seconds alone riding the elevator with the CEO and takes the opportunity to make a life-changing pitch.

In this moment, it became clear to Steve that he wanted to kick for the football team. So, he stood up as straight as he could and told Civetti, "Yeah. I kick."

As it turned out, Civetti was a graduate assistant, a coach who works while attending school to get his graduate degree. He was on his way to an evening class, Adolescent Psychology. He was running late, that's why he was cutting through the stadium, so he didn't linger very long.

"We've only got two kickers on the roster," Civetti said. "Are you interested?"

Steve didn't hesitate. "Dear God, yeah," he said. "Absolutely."

Civetti then told Steve to email Special Teams Coach Jerry Petercuskie and he would take it from there. Then Civetti turned, walked across the turf, and headed to his class.

As Civetti walked away, Steve posted up and kicked one more field goal. As soon as Civetti was out of sight, Steve ran all the way back to his dorm room, an uphill route all the way, and turned on his computer.

"Dear Coach Petercuskie. Today I met Coach Civetti who suggested I contact you. I'm a kicker…"

Chapter Six

Walking On

Although he never really officially tried out, Steve met with with Coach Jason Swepson, who handled the walk-ons, the next day, and as far as he knew, he was on the team. He couldn't attend practice until all the NCAA compliance paperwork was done, so that afternoon, Steve again went out by himself to kick on the field at the stadium. While he was kicking, Coach Petercuskie approached him.

"Are you Steve?" he asked.

"Yeah," said Steve.

"Do you have a kick-off tee?" Petercuskie asked.

"Yeah," said Steve.

"Alright," said Petercuskie. "Go back to the thirty and kick one."

So, he did, and according to Steve, he didn't do it very well. Then Coach Petercuskie, or Coach "Cuskie", as his players referred to him, called Steve over so they could talk.

"I asked where he was from," said Petercuskie. "He said, 'Easton, Pennsylvania.' Well, Easton High School is the only team that ever beat my dad's team when he coached at Neshaminy High School in Langhorne. So to start with, I liked that."

"I believe Coach Cuskie's dad was the winningest coach in Pennsylvania history," said Steve. "He went something like 62-1 at Neshaminy, and his one loss was to Easton! It was back in the '60's. My dad was a student at Easton at the time and remembers the game. It was an unbelievable connection."

Then Coach Cuskie asked Steve, "What else do you do?"

Steve told him he played baseball and soccer and they talked a little more.

Then Coach Cuskie cut the conversation short. "O.K., get some equipment and you can be on the team because you're a Pennsylvania boy."

And that was that.

Before he could formally join the team, Steve had paperwork to do and medical forms to provide. Because he had not expected to be playing football and since the season was already underway, he had to scramble to get them. So he called his parents.

According to Steve's mother, Jan, "Steve left a message on our machine that he was on the football team and he needed medical information so he could be cleared to play. Well, at first I thought, is he kidding? Why would he say a thing like that? Although, he's not really one to joke around that way. Then he left a fax number where we should send the forms. So, we thought, this must be for real."

Steve's sister, Kristin, remembers when Steve called to tell her and Jamie the news.

"Steve called and said, 'I'm on the football team at BC. I told him, 'That's nice. Does your dorm have a flag football team?' He'd never played football so I never in a million years would have thought he'd be on the actual football team. I just figured it was touch football or something. Then I asked him what position he would be playing! I had no clue."

Right away, Kristin called Jamie, who had spent many holidays and summer afternoons holding the ball for Steve as he kicked dozens of practice field goals and extra points.

"I was on the road for work and Kristin called me, all frantic," Jamie said. "I figured something was wrong, then she said, 'My brother made the football team!' It was out of nowhere but we thought it was incredible. Even though we figured he'd never play, it was thrilling for us just to know he'd be on the sidelines in a uniform. We were so excited just to hear that."

Next, Steve called his friend, Ian.

"He had called me the week before and told me he was going to go out and kick in the stadium," said Ian. "So, when he called a week later and said, 'You won't believe what happened,' I said, 'You got caught, didn't you? You broke in and campus police had to escort you out!' He says, 'No, not exactly.'"

Friends were emailing each other and spreading the word. Steve's friend, Pete Karch, said he heard the news on Facebook. And Ian said that before he even made a call, the phone chain had already begun. Maybe Steve's mom had told Brandon's mom because Ian called Brandon and then, Danny, they both answered the phone by saying, "Is it true?"

It was. Their friend was a Division I football player. For real. Well, almost. It would take a few days for all the compliance paperwork to be completed. So Steve, the new third-string, walk-on kicker for the Boston Eagles, had one more week as a civilian. BC had a home game against Army on Saturday, so there was just one thing to do. And it involved paint.

"I got to the game three hours before kickoff and painted my chest and all that," said Steve. "I didn't really know anybody yet so I was kind of by myself. But I found another kid who was interested in painting-up. I was the

'B' and he was the 'C'. So we just sat in the front row and started cheering."

Kevin Murphy, who became Steve's roommate and the football team's equipment manager the following year, was not the other painted- up fan, although he did sit with Steve at the game. He and Steve had just met, and to Steve's surprise, "Murph" was the only guy he could talk into going to the game several hours early.

"People don't take football as seriously in New England as we do in Pennsylvania," said Steve.

Probably true. Still, BC does have its own, enthusiastic student section where the majority of fans wear gold Superfan t- shirts, which were first worn en masse in 1997 when two students, Jeff Bridge and Chris Millette, spearheaded a campaign for fans to wear them to the BC vs. Virginia Tech game. Thinking he would lead this particular game's gold rush, Steve got an early start to the stadium, followed by Murph.

"We got to the game early, as soon as the gates opened," Murph said. "Steve was there, standing up with his fireman's helmet. He had a safari hat, too. Way before the game started, he starts chanting. 'Sixty minutes before Army gets their butt kicked!' Then a few minutes later, 'Fifty five minutes before Army gets their butt kicked!' He kept it up the entire game. I remember thinking, this kid is out there."

It was Steve's first and last game as a Superfan and the Eagles won it, (44-7).

The following week, Steve started practicing with the team. The first order of business was getting a uniform. Because he was a walk-on and because he was so late in joining the team, there were very few numbers left for him to choose from. Steve didn't care. His #83 jersey and the mismatched #111 sweatpants suited him just fine.

Next, he needed to be fitted for pads. Because he'd never played football before, Steve had never been fitted for football pads. In fact, once he got them, he didn't even know how to put them on.

"When you start with the team you can't wear pads for three or four practices so I had a chance to see how other guys were wearing them," Steve said. "I'd kind of watch everybody else and pass it off like I knew what I was doing. Luckily, it was pretty self-explanatory. Plus, kickers don't wear as much padding as some other positions."

Even so, the pads took some getting used to.

"It was weird at first," said Steve. "I had been kicking field goals on my own for years but never while wearing a five-pound helmet or five-pounds worth of shoulder pads. It's definitely different. I thought I was going to fall over every time I kicked."

Immediately, Steve got into the routine of practice. On weekdays during football season, the kickers normally had a special teams meeting at 2:00. They'd finish by 2:30 and head out to the field to "early kick" before the official practice began. They would kick a few field goals and the punters would punt. Then, when the rest of the team arrived on the field, Steve and the other kickers would hit kickoffs to the return men so they could work on catching kickoffs.

"That was sort of why I was brought on the team, to allow the return men to work on returns," said Steve. "Or, I'd play wide receiver on the scout team. There were times when they just needed bodies to line up at a position and I'd just go line up."

At practice, it was easy to identify the players on the scout team. They were the guys wearing gold jerseys, versus the white jerseys for the starting offense and the maroon jerseys for starting defense. Scout players often played the part of opposing players from the team BC would be playing that week. They even wore the opposing players' numbers on their gold jerseys.

On game day, the scout team would look for the players they had represented in practice.

"Our biggest satisfaction was watching those players get shut down by one of our guys," said Steve.

As a player on the scout team he was going up against first team defensive players. He'd never played football and now he was mixing it up with Division One athletes. At his first team physical, he weighed 158 pounds.

"Steve was not a big guy," said Ian McCutcheon. "In the real world he's an average-sized guy and now he'd be sticking his nose in there with these guys that were two heads taller and outweigh him by 250 pounds. It was hilarious. When I went to visit we'd hang out with the other guys on the football team and I thought, are these people even real? I was in an elevator with Steve and two defensive linemen and I was pretty sure the elevator wasn't going up."

Luckily for Steve, the coaches are well aware of the size differential.

"They don't really tackle at practice," said Steve. "And they would usually try to make sure the play was going away from my side. But I got hit a couple of times. Sometimes you couldn't help but get stuck in the mix."

His first hard knock came courtesy of linebacker Jo-Lonn Dunbar, a fierce defensive competitor who referred to Steve as "AP" and later would become a close friend.

"It was the week before we played Virginia Tech my freshman year," said Steve. "Usually I'd be the widest receiver and the play would be going the other way, but Virginia Tech ran this bunch formation with three receivers very close to the line. I had to go across the middle of the field and Joey just gave me a little push. All 160 pounds of me went flying about five yards."

If there is a lowliest position in all of sports, it just may be that of the college football walk-on.

Walk-ons are the aspiring players who come out to football practice in the fall (or sometimes the spring) and try-out for the team. Usually this happens after classes have already started and the scholarship players have been practicing together for weeks.

Walk-ons have an almost impossible bill to fill. First, they are competing for one of very few open spots on the roster. Then, in the unlikely event they make the team, walk-ons play as non-scholarship athletes. In other words, walk-ons pay for their tuition themselves while meeting the same requirements (maintaining a minimum GPA, attending all practices, following team rules) asked of their scholarship teammates.

Plus, walk-ons have to take a lot of crap. Often, these players are the grunts of the team who serve as opponents for their teammates during practice drills. Basically, they are warm bodies or tackling dummies whose job is to help the starting players prepare for games.

Walk-ons who make the team are almost always second, third or even fourth string players who are unlikely to see any real playing time. They are the reserves behind the reserves, many of whom don't travel to away games or dress for home games.

Why would anyone want to be a walk-on? For some players, this is their only shot at a lifelong dream to play college football. Walk-ons are often glass half-full guys, like Rudy Ruettiger from the beloved movie, *Rudy*. These guys are so passionate about football that they are willing to persevere despite the chance that they may never get to play in an actual game. Inspiring? Yes. A little crazy? Definitely.

Despite the long shot odds, there have been quite a few successful walk-ons over the years. Thanks to the movie which was based on his true experience at Notre Dame, Daniel Eugene "Rudy" Ruettiger is probably the best known. Rudy, a high school football player who grew up in Joliet, Illinois in the early 1970's had a two-part dream: to attend Notre Dame and to play football for the Fighting Irish.

Despite many obstacles including his diagnosis of dyslexia, Rudy persisted and after completing two years at nearby Holy Cross Junior College, he got the grades to transfer to Notre Dame. He then walked on to the football team and after spending two seasons playing his guts out in practice, he got the chance to dress for the final game of his senior year. Then, as the movie memorably portrayed, Coach Dan Devine finally put him in the game during the last two plays. After making a successful tackle as the clock ran out and the Irish won the game, his teammates carried Rudy off the field on their shoulders and a legend was born.

Besides Rudy, who went on to become a well-known inspirational speaker and book author, there have been other memorable college football walk-ons over the years.

Louis Oliver walked on to Coach Galen Hall's Florida Gators team in 1985. He not only became the starting free safety and earned a scholarship, but also was named team captain and won first-team All America honors in 1987 and 1988.

Andre Wadsworth walked on to Gators' rival Florida State's team in 1994. He not only earned a spot as a defensive tackle, but earned All-ACC honors during all four years he played for the Seminoles.

Another Florida-based player, Santana Moss, walked on to the Miami Hurricanes squad in 1997 where he became the school's leader in receiving yards (2,546) and all-purpose yards (4,393) before his college playing days were done.

Some walk-ons have not only excelled in college, but have defined the odds by going on to play in the NFL. One recent success story is Clay Matthews, the current Green Bay Packers standout linebacker.

Matthews (actually Clay Matthews III) played for his Agoura Hills, California high school team but was undersized and didn't start until his senior year after he finally began to grow and develop physically. After high school, Matthews decided to follow family tradition by attending the University of Southern California (USC), but unlike his four-year letterman father, Clay Matthews, Jr., and his three-year letterman uncle, Bruce Matthews, Matthews was not recruited and began his football career in 2004 as a walk-on.

Things turned around for Matthews, though, who earned a scholarship after his second year on the team and like his father, grandfather, and uncle, went on to play in the NFL.

The accomplishments of his father (who played the third most games in NFL history, 278, over nineteen seasons playing linebacker for the Cleveland Browns and Atlanta Falcons), and his uncle (nineteen-year Houston Oilers/ Tennessee Titans offensive lineman and 2007 Pro Football Hall of Fame inductee), will be tough to top but Matthews may be on his way. During his rookie season of 2009, Matthews was selected for the Pro Bowl, the first Packers rookie to earn the distinction since receiver James Lofton in 1978. He also now wears a Super Bowl ring following the Packers' victory in 2011.

Back in the late 1970's, defensive lineman Karl Mecklenburg walked on at The University of Minnesota, went on to become a two-time second team All-Big Ten selection and in 1983 he was a twelfth round draft pick for the Denver Broncos. He not only played in the pros, but this former walk-on went on to appear in six Pro Bowls and three Super Bowls.

Former Washington Redskins quarterback turned NFL free agent Colt

Brennan holds the distinction of having walked on to two different college football teams. First, in 2003, he walked on and played at the University of Colorado. Two years later he walked on at the University of Hawaii where during his senior season of 2008, he set the NCAA record for most touchdown passes in a single season, highest pass completion percentage and passing efficiency.

At Arizona State, there have been a string of walk-ons turned NFL pros including Darren Woodson, the linebacker who was named to five Pro Bowls and went on to win three Super Bowls while playing for the Dallas Cowboys from 1992-2004; Adam Archuleta, the star Pac-10 linebacker turned NFL safety who was drafted by the Rams in 2001; and Levi Jones, the Redskins' offensive tackle who was first drafted by the Cincinnati Bengals in 2002.

Brandon Burlsworth, a walk-on for the Arizona Razorbacks in 1996, became a second-team All America in college and a third-round pick for the Indianapolis Colts in the pros. He also is the namesake of the newly dedicated Burlsworth Trophy, which will be awarded annually to a player who began his career as a walk-on.

When he walked onto the team in 2005, Steve Aponavicius wasn't thinking of trophies or awards or even playing in an actual game. He was just happy to be there. He knew the rough road that a walk-on faced.

"I have a soft spot for all our walk-ons because of the rigors of what they're required to do compared to the benefits they receive," said trainer Steve Bushee. "We get a lot out of them and I'm not sure how much they get out of us. But I do think that at BC, walk-ons are respected and valued."

Steve knew how important that walk-ons were to the team and he gladly accepted his role. He was grateful for it. And he was committed.

During those first couple of meetings and practices, Steve learned what was expected of him. He learned a lot about what he needed to do. He also quickly learned what not to do.

"After my first day of practice we were walking out and Coach O'Brien, our head coach, was sitting on a bench," Steve said. "As I walked by I said, 'Hey, coach.' And he just stared at me! I asked some of the guys about it later and they said, 'Oh, no. We don't talk to Coach O'Brien unless he talks to us.' O.K., I get it."

Despite the fact that his teammates might have perceived him as an interloper who had never even played the game, according to Steve, the BC players welcomed him immediately.

"Some of the older guys, especially Jamie Silva and Jo-Lonn Dunbar, (both who went on to play in the NFL), took me under their wing right away," said Steve. "Within the first couple of days, Jamie came up to me and Matt

Ryan came up to me. They were the team leaders. They had no reason to even talk to me! But they really cared and wanted me to do well not just for the team's sake, but for my own sake, too. It was really neat."

"I could tell Steve was a pretty good kid from the start," said Jamie Silva. "He was genuine and sincere. He cared about his teammates, so he wanted to learn more about everybody. He probably knew the high school of every person on the BC team. Who takes the time to learn where everybody's from? That to me was incredible."

Steve also got plenty of pointers from punter, Johnny Ayers, a true freshman who also played baseball for BC.

"Johnny would tell me little tricks to avoid being hit," Steve said. "It's amazing, when somebody decides to go for the kicker, they usually come full steam. But because they put their heads down so early and run from so far away, you can get out of the way. At the last second, you can just step to the side."

Some college kids, especially those who don't play sports, have the perception that student athletes, especially football players, have it easy. Special privileges. Better food. Better housing. No need to come to class. To some degree, these things may be true. But consider things from the perspective of a third-string, walk-on football player studying business and finance at Boston College.

"When I first found out he was on the team, I told him to go for it," said Steve's future roommate, Kevin Murphy. "I said, 'Cool! Go play football!' But I didn't realize until later all the time and effort that goes into playing college football. They have such a strict schedule: early lifting, practice, meeting, class, practice, meeting, eat, homework, bed. He'd be up at 5:00 in the morning. When the rest of us are just getting up at 11:00 to go to our first class, he's already done with half his day. He had a bunk in forced triple—three guys to a room. He'd come back and put sheets and comforters all around his bottom bunk so no light would get in and he could take a nap. It was like his bear cave."

One of the most challenging things for Steve, and many of the freshman (and mostly red-shirted) players, besides setting their clocks for 4:55 AM, was getting used to the intense conditioning schedule at BC.

"When you're a freshman and not actually playing yet, you lift five days a week," said Steve. "These are the guys who are going to be playing in two or three years so the coaches want to develop them when they aren't playing on Saturdays."

Steve was not new to weight training. He and Ian had started lifting years before when they had access to the facilities at Lafayette College.

"We started lifting in sixth grade," said Steve. "Way before kids should have been lifting! I remember I couldn't even bench the bar, which is just pathetic."

Steve kept weight training throughout high school, although according to him, he didn't notice a significant difference. He was always in good shape from playing soccer and baseball, but you could never call him a big or bulky guy. You still couldn't call him big or bulky in college, especially as compared to most of his teammates, but it was soon apparent that he was getting much bigger and much stronger.

"I must have put on fifty pounds that year," said Steve. "I was eating a lot and running a lot, doing sprint work. That helps build up leg muscle. I just started adding pounds very quickly.

I got stronger as a whole, but the weight was all in my legs. I couldn't find pants that fit."

Still, when it comes to kickers, bigger isn't always better.

"I wanted to work on leg strength of course," he said. "So we did a lot of explosive lifts to help build fast twitch muscles. But kicking is such a weird skill because it's the kind of thing, you can lift all the time but the strongest guys in the world may not be able to kick a football ten yards. It doesn't have that much to do with strength. You need to develop fast twitch muscles but more, it's technique, and making good contact. It's really the speed of your leg when you kick the ball, not necessarily the strength or the bulk."

At BC, the football players train in groups. During Steve's freshman year, he trained with the other walk-ons and the scholarship players who were not on the traveling team. Todd Rice, who was the strength and conditioning coach at the time, remembers the first time Steve's group came in.

"One of the things I would always joke about with my assistant coach, Craig Buckley, was how the walk-ons come and go," said Rice. "They think they want to play then they'll quit after a couple of days or maybe a month. They're transient guys. They can be in and out so we nickname them to help us remember their names. So, we're going through the roll call and I looked at Steve's last name and said, there's no way this is spelled right. I asked Steve, how do you say this? He said, 'Aponavicius.' I said, 'What?' He said, 'Aponavicius.' I said, 'Oppa-what? Vicious?'"

Steve, who was very accustomed to this line of questioning, just grinned.

"Okay," said Rice. "Let's go, *Sid Vicious…*"

All the players and coaches cracked up. And when everybody laughs, a name is likely to stick. This one definitely did.

For his part, Steve didn't mind the name.

"You could have called me anything that first year and I wouldn't have minded," said Steve. "I was just so happy to be there."

But Sid Vicious? Steve admits that later that day, he went home and googled the name to find out exactly who this guy was.

"I knew he was some punk rock guy," said Steve, who was born seven years after Vicious died of a heroin overdose in 1979. "But I couldn't have told you he played bass for the Sex Pistols or that he was accused of killing his girlfriend and all that stuff."

So, with his teammates and coaches now referring to him as "Sid" or "Vicious", Steve got to work. The high standards he set for himself and his excellent work ethic were apparent from the start.

"A lot of times, kickers are kind of persnickety," said Coach Rice. "They want to be looked after and they're very concerned about becoming too bulky or losing flexibility. But with Sid, he always worked at what the rest of the team was working on whether it was learning how to squat or doing Olympic lifts, or cleans. He was such a regular, coming in the weight room a couple times a day. He was one of our most consistent guys and one of our most hardworking guys. That got him the respect of his teammates for sure."

"If there was conditioning going on and kickers didn't have to do it, he would do it anyway," said Jamie Silva. "He would be there every day. That was his work ethic and his way of being more a part of the team than he already was."

"It's a real testament to him that he just kept working and working and watching himself on film and taking little pointers from (starting kicker) Ohliger and myself," said Johnny Ayers. "He just slowly started improving, going from not working out in the weight room to working out five times a week. You can't do anything but improve when you're doing that."

Boston College Football - A Gridiron History

Football Saturdays and thrilling Thursday night games have come to be part of life at Boston College. Today, the Eagles are a consistently top-ranked football team competing in the Atlantic Coast Conference against formidable opponents including Virginia Tech, Maryland and Clemson. At home, the Eagles play at Alumni Stadium where they are cheered by as many as 44,500 fans who watch the action on the state of the art Field Turf field and catch replays on huge Jumbotron screens. Their games are broadcast nationwide to millions of viewers on TV; some fans even pick up the games on the internet or check their iPhones for text message updates during games.

But it wasn't always this way.

Like every college football program in the country, BC's gridiron history had humble beginnings. It all began in 1891 when Boston College President Edward I. Devitt, S.J., gave the student body permission to organize a football team.

To put things in historical perspective, in the early 1890's, Benjamin Harrison was the president of the United States, women still did not have the universal right to vote, Idaho and Wyoming were brand new states, and the first gas-powered automobile was yet to be introduced.

The concept of organized sports, especially in schools, was still very young. In fact, many sports, including basketball, which was invented by Dr. James A. Naismith in 1891, were just getting started.

Football was no exception. Despite the fact that the game looked a lot more like rugby than the gridiron football of today, the first official college football game is said to have been played between Princeton and Rutgers in New Brunswick, New Jersey on November 6, 1869. (Rutgers won, 6-4).

The game was controversial in its early, evolving form. In a newspaper story from the day there is an account of a professor from Rutgers passing by on his bicycle, who stopped to watch the milestone match for a moment and didn't like what he saw. "You men will come to no Christian end!" he shouted, before pedaling away.

Despite its reputation as dangerous and unruly, football began to catch on and colleges, mostly in the northeast, began to field teams.

Just over a decade later, in 1891, the first-ever Army-Navy game was played at West Point (Navy won 24-0). The same year, over at Boston College, twenty students came out to join the varsity football team.

Although according to *Boston College Football Vault: The History of the Eagles,* by author and former BC Director of Sports Media Relations, Reid Oslin, no money was allotted by the administration for a field, coaching staff, uniforms, equipment or medical care, the team began meeting that fall for practices. Joseph F. O'Connell, the student from BC's Class of 1893 who along with another student, Joseph C. Drum ('94), convinced the president to give permission for the team, was named captain and the following year when the squad began playing practice games he was named "coacher" as well.

The following season, a team of twenty-one players coached by Drum (O'Connell had graduated), gathered for their first practice in early October. Later that month, they played their first game against St. John's Literary Institute, a club team, who they beat 4-0. (Note: at the time, touchdowns were worth four points and points after touchdown were worth two points).

BC's first official intercollegiate game was played the following week against the Massachusetts Institute of Technology's freshman squad. Although the game was only partially played -- the teams were kicked off the field at halftime to make room for a Boston Athletic Association match against Harvard—the halftime score of 6-0 stood and M.I.T. was counted as winner.

The 1893 season wrapped when BC played Boston University, the beginning of a cross-town rivalry that would go on for decades.

In 1894, BC hired William Nagle from Mt. St. Mary's College in Maryland to coach the team. They even paid him a salary. The team also began wearing uniforms which consisted of football pants and boldly striped jackets and socks in the school's newly official colors, maroon and gold.

Despite the coach, the uniforms and a new fight song, *For Boston,* written by T.J. Hurley of the Class of 1885, the team won only one game that season.

In 1896, one of Boston College's major rivalries emerged when the football team played Holy Cross for the first time on their home turf in nearby Worcester, Massachusetts. BC won the scrappy game (6-2) after Holy Cross fumbled in the endzone. Later in the season, the two schools met again, this time at BC's field at the South End Grounds. Boston College won the second matchup as well (8-6), but the game, which is remembered for a major on-field melee and a BC score following a play that wasn't officially blown dead by the official-- remained controversial throughout the nearly one-hundred-year rivalry between the two schools.

The 1899 season was the team's best year to date. Not only did the squad finish the season 8-1-1, but it did so courtesy of nine shutouts and a thrilling victory (17-0) over Holy Cross during a season finale cheered by a BC home crowd of 6,000. Despite the incredible showing, the school's administration dropped football in 1900, due to financial constraints. The players still practiced together, though, and even played a few games, paying their own road expenses.

In 1901, the team was officially back but unfortunately, the momentum was lost as BC won one and lost eight that year.

At the turn of the century, college football looked a lot different than it does today. Players wore few if any pads and no helmets, just the thin leather caps that really just kept them warm and covered their ears. The rules and style of play were different, too.

One popular maneuver of the day was "the flying wedge," where players held hands or locked arms and charged at the opposition full speed, protecting the ball-carrier by surrounding him inside a pocket. Serious injuries piled up and the formation and the game itself was becoming more and more controversial. As a result, football programs were suspended by dozens of schools, including Boston College, which once again dropped the team in 1903.

A period of reform in the college game followed, with intervention by none other than President Teddy Roosevelt, whose son was a football player at Harvard.

In 1905 the Intercollegiate Athletic Association of the United States, which later became the National Collegiate Athletic Association, (NCAA), was formed and in 1906, the forward pass was legalized, which changed the dynamics of the game. In 1908, BC re-upped its football team.

As exciting as the games could be, conditions were far from glamorous for pioneering college football players. In the early 1900's, the BC squad practiced on the Massachusetts Avenue Grounds, the former site of a city dump where before practice each week, the players were required to mow the grass and line the field before running their drills.

Conditions improved in 1913 when the college moved from Boston's South End to its new and present location in Chestnut Hill, Massachusetts. After the move, players practiced at a nearby public park in Cleveland Circle. It was a mile-long walk to and from practice and according to *Boston College Football Vault,* they had to change into their gear in the basement of the Tower Building. At least they didn't have to do yard work.

As for games, the setting was somewhat more impressive, especially the following year when BC played two games at Fenway Park, the new Boston Red Sox stadium that opened in 1912. Some 8,000 fans showed up for the Thanksgiving Day game at Fenway to watch BC beat Catholic University (14-0).

By 1915, a new athletic field had been built on the site of a converted former piggery, part of the former Lawrence farm, a sprawling parcel of land that was sold to Boston College a few years prior. New Alumni Field, or Alumni Stadium, as it was also referred to, was located on the site of today's campus green and accommodated over 2,200 cheering fans.

In 1916, football at BC seemed to be garnering respect as the team staged its first-ever spring practice and hired a new coach, Charles Brickley, a former Harvard star player known for his recruiting abilities.

Then, in 1917, many college students left to join the army and fight overseas during World World I, or The Great War, as it was called at the time. Understandably, even though a schedule of games was played that fall, football was essentially put on the back burner.

When the war was over, BC hired a war hero, Frank Cavanaugh (known as "The Iron Major"), as coach. He stayed for eight seasons coaching star players such as punter, place-kicker, passer and runner, Jimmy Fitzpatrick; end Luke Urban, BC's first All-America player; and running back Al Weston.

In 1921, the newly-named Boston College Eagles were honored by being invited to play Baylor in the new Cotton Bowl stadium. BC not only accepted the offer and made the 2,300-mile train trip to Texas, but they beat Baylor handily, (23-7).

From 1919-1926, the Iron Major accumulated a record of 48-14-5, the longest run and best winning percentage of a Boston College football coach to date. Long after he left BC, his story was immortalized in a 1943 movie, *The Iron Major*, starring Pat O'Brien.

Cavanaugh was succeeded as head coach by former BC player, D. Leo Daley in 1927. Then, in 1928, Joe McKenney took over. The Eagles went undefeated (9-0) that year and played six more winning seasons under the leadership of their popular coach.

In the mid-late 1930's, BC's football program, which for three years (1936-38) was led by future College Football Hall of Fame Coach Gilmour Dobie, saw several milestones including the addition to the roster of the school's first African-American player, halfback Lou Montgomery. Incredibly, under the rules of the day, Montgomery was forbidden to play in games against Southern teams.

On a more positive note, in 1938, BC played its first game against a Big Ten team (BC: 14, Indiana: 0), and also played its first night game under lights – although the bulbs flickered on and off during a rainstorm. On New Year's Day 1940, BC played its first-ever post-season game when the Eagles met Clemson in the Cotton Bowl in Dallas, Texas. (Clemson won, 6-3).

The bowl game capped off a 9-1 season, the first under Coach Frank Leahy, a former Fordham assistant coach who, along with former BC head coach Cavanaugh, helped guide Fordham's "Seven Blocks of Granite" to great success. Leahy, a former Knute Rockne-coached player, introduced a Notre Dame box offense to BC, and the maroon and gold ran with it the following year as well, where they went undefeated (10-0) and finished the regular season ranked No. 4 in the national polls.

The grand finale of the 1940 season was the Sugar Bowl in New Orleans on January 1, 1941, where the Eagles faced-off against the Tennessee Volunteers, a team that had not lost a regular season game in three years. In front of a record-breaking crowd of 73,181 fans and thousands of listeners on the national radio broadcast, BC bested the Vols in the final three minutes of a previously 13-13 tie game courtesy of a touchdown run by Chuckin' Charlie O'Rourke. (Final score: BC: 19, Tennessee: 13).

Following the triumph in New Orleans, the so-called "Team of Destiny" boarded the train to Boston where over one hundred thousand fans greeted them at South Station. Many BC fans consider this team, which counted five future College Football Hall of Famers on its roster, as the best ever. In fact, although it was not officially named so by the national polling organizations at the time, and is not listed as such in NCAA records, many fans refer to 1940 as Boston College's National Championship season.

Although Coach Leahy left after the Sugar Bowl to accept the head coach position at Notre Dame, the winning tradition at BC continued under Coach Denny Myers. In 1942, approaching their final game against arch-rival Holy Cross, the Eagles were undefeated and ranked No. 1 in the country. But Holy Cross upset BC; the final score: 55-12.

As an oft-told story goes, BC players and fans were so demoralized following the loss to Holy Cross that they skipped a planned victory party at Cocoanut Grove, a restaurant in Boston. The cancellation of the celebration turned out to be a blessing since the venue was destroyed that night by a horrific fire where nearly five hundred people were killed.

The Orange Bowl on January 1, 1943 where BC made a good showing but ultimately lost to Alabama (37-21), would be the last bowl game the maroon and gold would play for nearly forty years.

Much like the teams in previous war years, BC's squads of the mid-1940's were greatly affected by World War II due to players leaving the Heights to serve in the army. Other considerations, such as travel restrictions on the home front, also came into play. But soon enough, after the war's end, life throughout the country and on college campuses would return to normal, and football would once again regain its front and center role.

Even though the original Alumni Stadium had been rebuilt in 1932, increasing its seating capacity to 12,500 with an additional 3,500 seats added the following year, during the era just before, during and after the war, Boston College played most of its biggest crowd-drawing "home" football games at larger and more accessible Boston venues such as Fenway Park or Braves Field, today's Nickerson Field on the Boston University campus.

According to *History of Boston College: From the Beginnings to 1990,* all Eagles home games from 1953-1956 were played at Fenway Park. Then, after the 1956 season, Boston Red Sox owner, Tom Yawkey, decided that football games would no longer be permitted at Fenway Park due to the wear and tear of the players' cleats on the turf.

With no adequate venue for the team, fans feared the football program might be dropped. In fact, the local *Boston Record* was so sure of the team's demise that they ran a "Dewey Defeats Truman" style erroneous headline, *BC Drops Football* the morning before BC President Joseph R.N. Maxwell, S.J. announced a new campaign to build a new, bigger, better stadium on the Boston College campus. Football was alive and well at BC.

The $250,000 Alumni Stadium Fund Drive, led by Athletics Director William J. Flynn and former BC coach turned Hall of Fame college football referee, Joe McKenney, was a success. Students and alumni volunteers not only pledged and raised money, but many pitched in as volunteers.

According to *Tales from the Boston College Sideline,* some students, including members of the football team, were hired as $1.38-an-hour laborers and incredibly, construction on the new 26,000 seat wood and steel stadium located on Boston College's lower campus, was completed in just 156 days.

A sellout crowd packed Alumni Stadium for the season opener in 1957, a BC-Navy matchup in part put together by then-U.S. Senator from Massachusetts, John F. Kennedy, who had served in the navy during World War II with BC Head Coach Mike Holovak. Unfortunately for BC fans, Navy stole the show with a 46-6 win.

Fourteen years later, in 1971, Alumni Stadium was expanded to 32,000 seats and other improvements were made, including the installation of artificial turf and stadium lights. In 1988, coinciding with the construction of Conte Forum, the stadium was once again rebuilt, this time with the additions of amenities such as matching upper decks and a new press box. In 1994, the stadium was expanded once more to its current capacity of 44,500,

The improvements kept coming – more and better instant replay screens, the 2008 unveiling of the bronze "Hail Flutie" statue in front of Gate D—but like the view of the Boston skyline from the top of the grandstands, some things, mainly the proud Boston College tradition, haven't changed since the stadium was dedicated back in 1957.

Following the 1959 season in which BC finished 5-4, Coach Holovak resigned his position, leaving BC after nine years and an overall record of 49-29-3. From there, Holovak was hired by the Boston Patriots, where he led the team as head coach for eight years. Later, he became an executive for the Houston Oilers/Tennessee Titans, serving as general manager, director of player personnel and vice president.

Ernie Hefferle took over as BC's head coach in 1960, but left after two consecutive losing seasons. Pundits and historians pretty much agree that these years, and several to follow, were partly a result of the limited resources of BC's football program. True, the new stadium was a boon. But to some degree, BC's teams of this era were effectively playing hurt. For example, as noted in *Boston College Football Vault,* the team worked with a staff of four assistant coaches compared with other top programs, that worked with as many as nine.

Even so, the 1960's had its share of highlights (the 8-2 season of 1962 under Coach Jim Miller) and memorable games (the 21-14 last second upset of ninth-ranked Syracuse in 1964 and the 49-15 victory over Navy, the first win over the Midshipmen in 40 years, in 1968). But the decade also had its share of disappointments, such as the back-to-back 4-6 seasons of 1966 and 1967 and the November 23, 1963 game against Boston University that was cancelled due to the assassination of President Kennedy the day before. The game, which was never made-up, would have been the last game ever played between the two rivals.

In 1968, Coach Joe Yukica, who famously insisted on upgrades in the school's football staff and facilities, took the reins for what would become an impressive ten-season run. After a relatively slow start during his first two seasons, Yukica's team picked up steam and finished 8-2 and 9-2 in 1970 and 1971, respectively.

Of course there were talented players behind these wins, notably quarterback Frank "Red" Harris, who set passing yardage and touchdown records that would stand for a decade, and running back Fred Willis, who became BC's first player to surpass 1,000 yards in a single season.

The 1973 season was another winner for the maroon and gold. BC finished 7-4, and they did so courtesy of upsets and new precedents, including the September 29th come-from-behind win (32-24) over Texas A&M during BC's first-ever trip to College Station, Texas.

The Eagles, who stayed at a dude ranch the night before the game, got off to a rocky start when A&M's Carl Roaches caught the opening kickoff on his team's goal line and returned it one-hundred yards for a score. But BC battled back, scoring fifteen of their final thirty-four points in the last two-plus minutes of the game, which was BC's first win below the Mason-Dixon Line since 1962.

After the game, Coach Yukica, who was not known to be a screamer, stood on a chair in the middle of a rowdy-post game locker room and yelled, *"Men! Men! Men!"*

When he had their attention, he yelled even louder, *"The South is dead!"*

In 1974, the Eagles finished 8-3, a record to be proud of, but a closer look turns up some equally impressive stats. At one point during the season, the Eagles were on a roll, outscoring their opponents 270-27. Also of note, quarterback Mike Kruczek set an NCAA passing completion record that year by completing 104 of 151 throws for a stunning 68.9 completion rate. The previous record-holder, whose completion rate was 68.4 in 1962, was Navy's Heisman Trophy winner turned NFL star, Roger Staubach.

The 1975 season began with a bang when BC played Notre Dame for the first time, a match-up which that year, and during semi-regular meetings in subsequent years, has been dubbed, "The Holy War."

According to *Tales from the Boston College Sideline,* BC's first-ever nationally televised game, which was played at the 61,500-seat Schaefer Stadium in Foxborough, Massachusetts, was sold out nearly two years before the two future rivals ever hit the field. Over one hundred sportswriters covered the game, which was photographed from high above the stadium by the Goodyear Blimp. Despite all the hoopla, Notre Dame came out on top, beating BC (17-3).

Some of the most memorable Holy Wars over the years include the 1993 game where the Eagles beat the No. 1 – ranked Fighting Irish (41-39) on a last-second, forty-one yard field goal, wrecking Notre Dame's chance for a National Championship. The Eagles served as spoilers again in 2002 when they beat the previously undefeated Irish 14-7. The games in 2007 and 2008 also went BC's way: in 2007, BC's 27-14 victory marked the Eagles' first 7-0 season since 1942 as well as their fifth consecutive Irish defeat, and BC's 17-0 win in 2008 marked the first time either team was able to shut out its opponent.

The Eagles' successful 8-3 season of 1976 kicked-off with a thrilling 14-13 victory over No. 7- ranked Texas, thanks partly to the electrifying seventy-four yard touchdown sprint by running back Neil Green and a game-ending tackle by cornerback Kelly Elias.

The following year marked the end of Coach Yukica's tenure at BC, which was the longest and winningest of any coach in the program's history so far.

The fall of 1978 was one that BC fans would like to forget. Under Coach Ed Chlebek, the maroon and gold failed to win a game. The following two seasons were big improvements, (BC went 5-6 in 1979 and 7-4 in 1980), but despite winning six of his last seven games,

Chlebek moved on. In 1981, Coach Jack Bicknell was hired and a new era of BC football began.

A few years later, in 1984, one of the greatest games in college football history was played on Coach Bicknell's watch. It was the day after Thanksgiving and the BC Eagles were set to play the Miami Hurricanes at the Orange Bowl in Miami, Florida.

The teams were mostly an even match. The Eagles were 8-2 and ranked No.10 in the nation. The Hurricanes were 8-3 and ranked No. 12. If there was a slight edge, Miami, as home team and the defending national champs, could probably have claimed it. Plus, Miami's Coach Jimmy Johnson was fired up after his team squandered an enormous (31-0) early lead to lose to Maryland (42-40) the week before.

Regardless, most pundits agreed, it was anybody's game. And that's exactly how it went. Back and forth. BC broke out with an early 14-0 lead in the first quarter, but Miami quickly responded with two touchdowns to tie the game.

It quickly turned into an offensive shootout where Miami quarterback Bernie Kosar ultimately passed for 447 yards while BC quarterback Doug Flutie passed for 472. (Prior to that, no opposing quarterbacks had ever thrown for 300 yards each in the same game). The quarterbacks were setting records and the defenses on both sides seemed to be stopping nothing as the points piled up.

Then, with just over three minutes left to play in the fourth quarter and Miami leading 38-34, BC running back Steve Strachman ran four yards for a touchdown. The Eagles were up 41-38.

Soon, the Hurricanes got the ball back and Kosar led his team down field some seventy-eight yards to the BC one-yard line. With just thirty seconds left to play, Miami called timeout. Kosar ran to the bench and could be heard on national TV telling Coach Johnson, "We should just ram it down their ---- throats!"

Indeed, on the next play, Miami's Melvin Bratton jammed it in and scored his fourth touchdown of the day. It was Miami: 45 – BC: 41.

Miami kicked-off and with the clock running, BC ran it to the twenty-yard line. On the next play, Flutie passed to running back Troy Stradford for nineteen yards. Next, he hit tight end Scott Gieselmann for another eleven yards. Then, Flutie threw the ball out of bounds to stop the clock.

When the Eagles huddled up, Flutie called "55 Flood Tip" whereby three receivers run fly patterns down the right side.

With just six seconds to play, Flutie took the snap and scrambled as Stradford and Kelvin Martin sprinted down field and stopped at the five-yard line, with Miami's deep backs in hot pursuit, while Gerard Phelan ran to the end zone and cut back to the middle.

All the while, Miami defensive linemen were chasing Flutie who finally, from the Eagles thirty-yard line, launched a sixty-three-yard Hail Mary pass to Phelan, Flutie's roommate and best friend, who gathered the ball in his arms and tumbled into the endzone as the clock expired.

CBS Broadcaster Brent Musburger called the play this way: "Flutie flushed…throws it down…CAUGHT BY BOSTON COLLEGE! I don't believe it! It's a touchdown! The Eagles win it!"

The play, known ever since as *Hail Flutie,* has been immortalized in countless TV highlight clips; there's even a NCAA College Classic video game where players recreate the famous ending of the game. *Hail Flutie* is on everybody's list (Fox Sports' Ten Best Damn Unforgettable Sports Moments, ESPN's 100 Most Memorable Moments of the Past 25 Years and *Sports Illustrated's* Top 10 Scrambling Quarterbacks of All Time) as one of the greatest college football plays of all time. There is even a road named "Flutie Pass" in Flutie's hometown of Natick, Massachusetts. And perhaps the most lasting legacy of one Hail Mary pass was the surge in applications to Boston College, which even today, when colleges enjoy a spike in applications due to their athletic team's success on the field, is referred to as The Flutie Effect.

According to Reid Oslin, BC's Director of Sports Media Relations at the time, the effect still lingers.

"The whole level of competition was raised and the visibility that goes along with it," he said. "Flutie was a groundbreaker."

The thrilling final play sometimes overshadows what was overall, an absolutely incredible game that is continually replayed on ESPN Classic. During all four quarters of the Miracle in Miami, both sides piled up an impressive stack of statistics.

Phelan's game-winning catch was his eleventh catch of the game. Miami's Melvin Bratton scored four touchdowns, including a fifty-two yard run. Bernie Kosar's 447 passing yards included two touchdown passes for the Hurricanes. And in the course of throwing for 472 yards, Flutie became the first ten-thousand-yard passer in major college history.

One week later, Doug Flutie won the Heisman Trophy.

Although the miraculous spiral he threw to Gerard Phelan that day in Miami certainly didn't hurt his chances, Flutie was awarded the Heisman not because of one play, but rather, his win was based on four years of consistently outstanding performances.

BC's Flutie era began in 1981 when the young quarterback (and baseball and basketball standout) from Natick, Massachusetts turned down scholarship offers from Holy Cross and Syracuse, where football coaches intended for him to play defensive back. Instead, the Natick High School graduate came to BC, where he was recruited after an assistant coach, Barry Gallup, now BC's Associate Athletic Director for Football Operations, noticed him during BC's football day camp the previous summer and despite his small stature, saw enormous potential and sang his praises as a quarterback.

When Flutie signed with BC, new head coach Jack Bicknell assured him that he would eventually get the chance to play quarterback. As it turned out, Flutie's opportunity would come sooner than later.

Just prior to the start of the 1981 season, junior quarterback John Loughery tore his thumb ligaments in a pre-season practice and was sidelined for the first several games. The Eagles would be forced to face formidable foes, a line-up of teams nicknamed Murderer's Row, which included Texas A&M, North Carolina, West Virginia and No. 2 -ranked Penn State, without their starting quarterback.

As the coaches scrambled to find Loughery's replacement, freshman Doug Flutie played his first game as an Eagle when he was sent in for the final series against West Virginia, which beat BC (38-10).

The following game, Flutie logged more playing time when once again, he went in during the fourth quarter against Penn State. As soon as he hit the field, Flutie immediately got to work racking up 135 passing yards, which included a flawless touchdown pass to tight end Scott Nizolek for BC's only score of the game. Although Flutie's efforts weren't enough to garner a win, (Penn State beat BC, 38-7), it was impossible not to notice his performance.

According to *Boston College Football Vault: The History of the Eagles,* Coach Bicknell later commented on Flutie's debut.

"It was like someone threw a switch," said Bicknell. "It became obvious to me from that very moment on that the kid was special."

For the remainder of the season, and indeed, for the rest of his four-year college career, the starting quarterback job belonged to Flutie. Despite another Eagles loss (29-24) to Pittsburgh, led by quarterback Dan Marino, all eyes were on Flutie who passed for 347-yards. The Eagles picked up the pace and won four of their final six games of what ultimately became a 5-6 year with their young quarterback passing for two-hundred-plus yards each against Holy Cross, Syracuse, Army, and Massachusetts.

The Eagles fared better in 1982 when they won eight games, lost two and tied one. The 17-17 tie, against defending national champion Clemson, was a standout performance by Flutie where he completed eighteen of thirty-five passes for 242 yards. Several games later, Flutie and company engineered a down-to-the-wire, 14-13 comeback win over Rutgers, which could have been a dress rehearsal for the Miracle in Miami two years later.

The season finale was a visit to the Tangerine Bowl, the Eagles' first bowl game appearance in forty years. Although the Eagles lost to Auburn (33-26), Flutie was named game MVP, an honor he would claim again the following year in the Liberty Bowl against Notre Dame.

In 1983, the Eagles lost only two regular season games, to Syracuse and West Virginia. The wins were thrilling, often thanks to Flutie, especially the 31-16 drubbing of Clemson, the last-second 18-15 squeaker against Temple, and the 20-13 upset against heavily-favored Alabama, where the Eagles beat the Crimson Tide in the bitter cold following a dramatic forty-two-minute power blackout at Sullivan Stadium in Foxborough, Massachusetts.

Then, for the first time in school history, BC beat Penn State (27-17), and spent the rest of 1983 ranked in the Top 20.

Flutie's senior season of 1984 became the one that BC fans will never forget. For the second year in a row, the Eagles beat Alabama, this time in a come-from-behind 38-31 victory in Birmingham where in the second half Flutie scored on a five-yard touchdown run, hit fullback Jim Browne for a twelve-yard touchdown pass and pitched to Troy Stradford, who ran for a forty-three yard score.

The following week, Flutie delivered six touchdown passes in a 52-20 trouncing of North Carolina. BC fans watched in awe as Flutie again and again, scrambled out of harm's way, while the impressive offensive line, Mark MacDonald, Steve Trapilo, Jack Bicknell Jr., Mark Bardwell and Shawn Regent, nicknamed "the Secret Service," provided top-notch protection.

All season long, Flutie accumulated gaudy numbers, throwing four touchdown passes during the season opener against Western Carolina, and three a piece against Rutgers, Army and Holy Cross.

During his final home game at Alumni Stadium, Flutie broke college football's all-time career passing record of 9,614 yards formerly held by Duke's Ben Bennett, as BC defeated Army (45-31). Then the Eagles went on the road and after beating Syracuse (24-16), they headed south to play the now-famous game in Miami.

The Eagles went on to win their last regular season game of 1984, when they beat longtime rival Holy Cross (45-10). The game featured a Flutie first when the Eagles' star quarterback connected on a touchdown pass with his younger brother Darren, a freshman wide receiver.

Flutie finished the regular season having passed for 3,454 yards and twenty-seven touchdowns, both school records. Then the Eagles put a positive postscript on the season with a 45-28 victory over the Houston Cougars in the Cotton Bowl, BC's first New Year's Day bowl game in forty-two years. Despite a stormy, icy second half that kept the ball mostly on the ground, BC managed to tally some 533 yards of offense.

What a year. The Eagles finished their 9-2 season with a Cotton Bowl victory, a No. 4 (UPI) and No. 5 (AP) ranking and the honor of a lifetime for their quarterback when Doug Flutie became the first player in Boston College history (and the first quarterback since Pat Sullivan in 1971) to win the Heisman Trophy.

Flutie had come close to winning the Heisman the previous year when after the 1983 season he finished third in the polling after the winner, Mike Rozier of Nebraska, and first-runner up, Steve Young of Brigham Young. But in 1984 there was no doubt about who was not only the most exciting quarterback in the league but the nation's top college football player.

After collecting The Heisman, Flutie gathered armfuls of other honors including the Maxwell Award, which like the Heisman, is given to the nation's outstanding college football player; The Walter Camp Award, also given to the college football player of the year; the Davey O'Brien National Quarterback Award and many other player of the year awards including nods from the UPI, Kodak, and *The Sporting News*. He was also named to every major 1984 All-America team and honored back at BC with the Eagle of the Year Award, which is presented each year to the outstanding male and female athletes in the senior class. Plus, every kid in Boston was wearing a #22 jersey.

Flutie's academic achievements were also recognized when he won a National Football Foundation post-graduate scholarship and was nominated for a Rhodes scholarship.

Flutie won't soon be forgotten at BC. He finished with a major college career record of 10,579 yards and still holds many BC school records (Most TD's in a Game: 6, Most Yards in a Game: 520, Total Career Yards: 11,318).

After doing more than his fair share to help raise BC's profile on the national collegiate football stage, Flutie went on to play in the NFL. Just after graduation, he was selected by the Los Angeles Rams in the eleventh round of the National Football League (NFL) draft, but instead, he decided to sign with the New Jersey Generals of the United States Football League (USFL) and played for them for one season, after which the league folded.

Halfway through the 1986 season, Flutie signed with the Chicago Bears, then played for the New England Patriots for three years. His next stop in a pro career that ultimately lasted twenty years was the Canadian Football League where he excelled from the start. During his first season with British Columbia, he threw for 6,619 yards, a pro football record and won four straight Most Outstanding Player trophies.

Flutie returned to the NFL in 1998, and played for Buffalo, San Diego and New England until 2006, when he retired at the almost unheard-of-for-a-pro-football-player age of forty-three. After his playing days, Flutie became an ABC/ESPN college football analyst and has long been a fixture at BC's Alumni Stadium, where his retired #22 jersey hangs proudly.

Not surprisingly, the Flutie years were a near impossible act to follow and the team struggled in 1985, ultimately winning just four games. On the positive side that year, nose tackle and team captain Mike Ruth, a senior from Norristown, Pennsylvania, was honored with the Outland Trophy, an award presented annually to the nation's best interior offensive or defensive lineman.

When Ruth received this award, he raised the bar for future recipients: he was the first-ever honoree from a non-winning team. Of course, Ruth did play on successful teams his first three years, and he contributed mightily during each season.

On the field, Ruth was impossible to miss. The 6-1, 265-pound lineman piled up dozens of sacks and nearly three-hundred tackles during his career, beginning with his freshman year of 1982 when he made thirty-six tackles and three sacks when he was just a back-up player. During his sophomore year, Ruth more than doubled his numbers, playing consistently hard despite a season-long ankle injury. In 1984, he was effectively the key to BC's defense, bulldozing his way through opposing blockers to accumulate 102 tackles, seventy-six of them solo.

Off the field, Ruth was a soft-spoken guy who back home in Pennsylvania would sometimes carry his arthritis-afflicted mother to and from her pew when the family went to church. Ruth seriously considered going into the priesthood after college, but instead he went into the NFL after being drafted in the second-round and played for the New England Patriots during the 1986-87 season.

Eleven years later, Ruth's #68 was retired along with Doug Flutie's jersey, in a ceremony at Alumni Stadium.

Although 1986 was a winning year (9-3) for the maroon and gold, the next five seasons were disappointments regarding the final season tallies. One bright spot was the Emerald Isle Classic, a BC vs. Army game played in Dublin, Ireland in 1988. The exhibition, which BC won (38-24), was the first American college football game ever played in Europe.

In 1992, the Eagles turned things around with an impressive 8-3 season, the team's second year under head coach Tom Coughlin. The new boss was not exactly new to Chestnut Hill. He'd served as an assistant to Coach Jack

Bicknell for three seasons back in 1981-83 before heading to the NFL where prior to accepting the BC job, he worked as the Super Bowl Champion New York Giants' receivers coach under Bill Parcells.

When he returned to town, Coughlin had the exciting task of leading his team as a member of the just-formed Big East Football Conference, which along with Boston College included Temple, West Virginia, Rutgers, Virginia Tech, Miami, Syracuse, and Pittsburgh.

Coughlin was known for his precise nature (he would leave his home at exactly 5:20 AM every morning), his all-business approach (he had workmen paint a "Line of Concentration" at the entrance to the field), and his work ethic (he never missed a game even when he contracted pneumonia during the 1991 season).

Sadly for the Eagles, a cloud hung over the successful season of 1992 when in July of that year, defensive back Jay McGillis died of leukemia. The team paid tribute to their friend and teammate by wearing #31 patches on their uniforms throughout the following season.

Although the fall of 1993 got off to a rocky start when BC lost their first two games to Miami (23-7), and Northwestern (22-21), the team soon rallied with a string of eight unforgettable wins including their besting of No. 13-ranked Syracuse (33-29), a longtime rival, and No. 25 Virginia Tech (48-34), a new Big East and future Atlantic Coast Conference rival.

Perhaps sweetest of all was the last minute victory (41-39) over No. 1-ranked Notre Dame, a thrilling win, courtesy of kicker David Gordon's field goal, which foiled the previously perfect season for the Irish.

After wrapping the season with a win over Virginia (31-13) in the Carquest Bowl in Fort Lauderdale, Coach Coughlin left BC to return to the NFL as head coach of the expansion Jacksonville Jaguars.

In 1994, Doug Henning, a longtime NFL assistant and former head coach of the Atlanta Falcons and San Diego Chargers, took over as BC's head coach. The team faced enormous challenges that year, beginning with an intimidating schedule that began with Michigan and continued with a string of strong Big East opponents. Plus, Alumni Stadium was being completely renovated and as satisfying as the grand reopening would be, during the summer and pre-season, the team had to schedule 6:00 AM practices at Boston University's field.

After two consecutive losing seasons complete with many off-field distractions including an ugly betting scandal that resulted in the suspension of thirteen team members, Henning departed and Tom O'Brien, a Naval Academy graduate and longtime Navy and Virginia assistant coach, was hired as the Eagles' new on-field boss.

The O'Brien era, which ultimately would last a decade and feature some of BC's best teams, had a different vibe from the start. The no-nonsense, ex-military O'Brien instituted strict policies which according to *Boston College Football Vault: The History of the Eagles* included everything from collecting and holding players' car keys to eliminating team cliques.

Still, rebuilding takes time, and despite being led by future NFL star quarterback Matt Hasselbeck, who ultimately stacked up 4,548 career passing yards and won the George "Bulger" Lowe Award as New England's best player, the Eagles finished 4-7 in 1997.

In 1998, despite great performances by players such as running back Mike Cloud, who set the then-school record of 3,597 career rushing yards, the Eagles again finished 4-7. But that would be the last losing season for O'Brien's Eagles.

Beginning with 1999, BC notched eight consecutive winning seasons, each capped off by a post-season bowl bid. (The Eagles won seven of their eight bowl appearances during this stretch).

Soon, BC fans became accustomed to their team beating major players such as Notre Dame and Penn State as well as conference foes including Pittsburgh, Syracuse and West Virginia. It became commonplace at Alumni Stadium to see awesome performances by running backs such as Cedric Washington, who ran for 1,122 yards in 1999; and William Green, who ran for 1,164 yards in 2000 and 1,559 in 2001.

Certainly, there were losses and disappointments along the way. But as the millennium turned, excellence had become the on-field norm at BC.

In 2002, The Eagles lost games to Miami, Virginia Tech, Pittsburgh, and West Virginia, but the losses (four) were outnumbered by the wins (nine), which tended to share a lop-sided quality.

The exception was the thriller against Notre Dame where unranked BC beat the No. 4-ranked Irish (14-7) in South Bend. The show was dominated by linebacker Josh Ott's interception and subsequent seventy-one yard score, as well as his fumble recovery and fifteen tackles. The finale came courtesy of Sandro Sciortino's twenty-six yard field goal as the clock ran out.

The following season, BC finished 8-5, notching, among others, a memorable win against Virginia Tech (34-27), the Eagles' first defeat of the Hokies in seven years. During this win, running back Derrick Knight not only piled up 197 yards and two touchdowns, but he also set the mark as BC's all-time leading rusher (3,725 yards).

Also in 2003, Boston College President Rev. William P. Leahy, S.J., and Director of Athletics Gene DeFilippo announced that as of 2005, teams at BC would compete as part of the Atlantic Coast Conference (ACC).

"The ACC is a strong, stable conference, and membership in it secures the future of our intercollegiate athletic conference," Leahy said. "Our decision to join the Atlantic Coast Conference is based on my judgment of what's best for us academically, athletically and financially."

The announcement of the conference switch put the spotlight on games against Big East opponents in 2004, especially the match-ups with West Virginia and Syracuse, which unlike Miami and Virginia Tech, would not be making the move to the ACC.

In Morgantown, the Eagles trounced the Mountaineers (36-17), after cornerback DeJuan Tribble set the tone in the first quarter with a forty-one-yard punt return. But two weeks later in Chestnut Hill, BC fans were disappointed when Syracuse came out on top (43-17). There was one consolation, though. The game marked the debut of a new quarterback, Matt Ryan, who came in for the first time to replace the injured Paul Peterson (likely the only Mormon ever to play quarterback for a Jesuit school).

In 2005, The Eagles were not only playing as part of a new conference, but at home they were practicing at a gorgeous new, twenty-seven million dollar facility, the Yawkey Center. Ironically, the facility, which was largely funded by a grant from the Yawkey Foundation, is named after Tom Yawkey, the former Boston Red Sox owner who pulled the plug on college football games at Fenway Park back in the early 50's.

At game time, it appeared as though BC had arrived when the team played their first-ever ACC matchup against Florida State, a lively event covered by ESPN's College Game Day crew in its inaugural visit to Alumni Stadium. Although the No.8-ranked Seminoles beat the No.17 Eagles (28-17) that day, BC went on to be nationally ranked each week and win nine games that year.

Among the highlights of the 2005 season was the victory (35-30) over Wake Forest in Chestnut Hill when in the fourth quarter, Matt Ryan came off the bench to engineer a magnificent comeback. With only 2:18 left to play, Ryan connected on seven of nine passes for 134 yards and two touchdowns, the first a thirty-eight yard bullet to wide receiver Tony Gonzalez; the second a twenty-six yarder to Kevin Challenger. A sign of things to come.

The Eagles kicked-off the 2006 season with a win (31-24) over Central Michigan, followed by two more victories, both double overtime nail biters over Clemson and BYU. Next, unranked NC State upset the No. 2- ranked BC (17-15) with a last minute, Doug Flutie-style "Hail Mary" touchdown. The Eagles regrouped, though, and served up four wins in a row, including a thrilling 22-3 victory over Virginia Tech, where walk-on kicker Steve Aponavicius went four-for-four (two field goals, two extra points) in his successful debut.

Despite finishing the season with a winning record of 10-3, losses to Wake Forest and Miami ruined BC's shot at an ACC Championship. This disappointment—and the lack of invitations to big time bowls over the last few seasons -- put a cloud over the tremendous achievements of head coach Tom O'Brien, who in ten years, won more games (75 wins, 45 losses) than any coach in Boston College history.

At season's end, Coach O'Brien accepted the job as head coach at NC State and BC assistant coach, Frank Spaziani, was named interim coach for the Meineke Car Care Bowl on December 30th in Charlotte. Spaziani rose to the enormous challenge of quickly uniting a team under a new head coach and preparing them to play Navy, a team known for their complicated triple-option attack.

The game turned out to be a dog fight with Navy edging slightly ahead in the fourth quarter. With just two minutes remaining, the Midshipmen were up 24-22 when BC linebacker Jo-Lonn Dunbar recovered a fumble at Navy's thirty-six yard line. Then, Matt Ryan moved the Eagles down field and set up a thirty-seven-yard, game-winning field goal by Aponavicius as time ran out. A thrilling end to the season and the perfect set-up for the following fall.

In 2007, the Eagles played their best season in recent memory, lining up nothing but W's from the start with victories over Wake Forest, NC State, Georgia Tech, Army, Massachusetts, Bowling Green, and Notre Dame. By the time they traveled to noisy Lane Stadium in Blacksburg to take on Virginia Tech, the Eagles were ranked No.3 in the nation.

Late in the game, the home crowd was raucous as the clock wound down with the Hokies ahead (10-0). Then, with just over two minutes to play, Matt Ryan threw a sixteen-yard touchdown pass. The Eagles followed by recovering an onside kick to set up another score, this one a 24-yard toss to tailback Andre Callender, one of many that year that ultimately earned him BC's single-season reception record (76).

Following the Virginia Tech win, Boston College was ranked No. 2 in the nation, their highest standing in the polls since 1942. The top-ranked Eagles shook off losses to Florida State and Maryland, and soon enough, were back in form for another come-from-behind victory (20-17) over conference rival Clemson. Then after beating Miami for the first time in over a decade, BC was bound for the ACC-Championship and a re-match against Virginia Tech.

This time, the Hokies prevailed (30-16), but it was impossible to throw a wet blanket on the 2007 season, the first led by Head Coach Jeff Jagodzinksi.

The maroon and gold won eleven games, the most of any BC team since 1940, capping the year with a 24-21win over Michigan State at the Champs Sports Bowl in Orlando. The bowl victory marked BC's eighth consecutive post-season win.

As for Matt Ryan, at the end of his senior year of 2007, he was a Heisman trophy contender who collected a slew of honors including The

George "Bulger" Lowe Award (which he shared with BC defensive back Jamie Silva), and ACC Player of the Year. He also set school records for all-time single-season passing yards (4,507), single-season touchdown passes (31), and career completions (807), before leaving Chestnut Hill.

In 2008, Ryan was selected by the Atlanta Falcons third overall in the first round of the NFL Draft. After his first pro season, Ryan was named 2008 NFL AP Offensive Rookie of the Year and after his third successful season leading the Falcons, he was elected to the 2011 Pro Bowl. No one doubts that Ryan will have a long, exciting career in the NFL and Eagles' fans will never forget where he got his start.

Back at Boston College, 2008 was another celebratory season for the Eagles. The long win column included victories over NC State (38-31), Florida State (27-17) as well as a 17-0 victory at Alumni Stadium over Notre Dame, BC's sixth consecutive defeat of the Fighting Irish.

At season's end, the Eagles once again played –and lost (30-12)—to Virginia Tech in the ACC Championship Game. (Hence, the rivalry).

Also, following the 2008 season, junior linebacker Mark Herzlich was named ACC Defensive Player of the Year and was a finalist for the Butkus Award, presented annually to the nation's top college linebacker. No one who witnessed Herzlich's exciting on-field performances including thirteen tackles against Georgia Tech and Virginia Tech; two interceptions against Wake Forest; and seven stops against the Hokies during the ACC Championship game was surprised that he was so honored.

There was talk that he would skip his senior year and head straight to the NFL but Herzlich shocked many of his teammates and fans by electing to stay and finish school before going pro. Then, he again shocked – no, stunned – everyone when in the spring of 2009, Herzlich announced that he had been diagnosed with Ewing's Sarcoma, a rare form of bone cancer.

Although Herzlich missed the entire 2009 season due to his illness, he again astonished his teammates and college football fans everywhere by announcing in October of '09 that he was cancer-free.

Herzlich not only returned to the BC line-up in 2010 for his postponed senior year, but he excelled, finishing third on the team in total tackles (65) and solo stops (50), while leading the Eagles in forced fumbles (2). Along with his teammate, left tackle, Anthony Castonzo, Herzlich played in the 2010 senior bowl and as of 2011, is NFL-bound.

Perhaps his most lasting legacy, besides the hundreds of thousands of dollars raised in his name for cancer research, was the inspiration he provided and left behind with the Boston College community.

At the beginning of the 2009 season, besides the good news about

Herzlich, Eagles fans were celebrating the debut of their new head coach, Frank Spaziani. The new boss had an advantage as he took over at BC: with his win while serving as BC's interim head coach in the 2006 Meineke Bowl, Spaziani had a perfect record as a head coach. Plus, he had serious football credibility going back to his college days at Penn State where he played running back and defensive end and then worked as a graduate assistant for Coach Joe Paterno.

Spaziani had also worked under Head Coach George Welsh for 15 years at Navy, then at Virginia. After that, he spent five years as an assistant coach in the Canadian Football League before coming to Boston College where he coached running backs for two years and served as defensive coordinator for nine years.

With Spaziani at the helm, the Eagles finished 8-5 in 2009. A particular high point that season was the Halloween game against Central Michigan. Not only did the Eagles win it (31-10), but during the course of the victory, kicker Steve Aponavicius surpassed kicker Brian Lowe (1986-89) and his former points record of 262 to become BC's all-time scoring leader with 267 points.

The 2010 season was especially challenging as the injury-plagued-Eagles finished 7-6. Still, BC showed their stuff when after a string of losses, players such as linebacker, Luke Kuechly, the leading tackler in the nation and running back, Montel Harris, the ACC's leading rusher, helped make BC the first team in ACC history to win five consecutive games after losing five in a row. The Eagles also led the nation in rushing defense and played in their twelfth straight bowl game.

Regarding the future, no one knows what great gridiron achievements are yet to come. Just as the two students who started it all over a century ago could never have dreamed of a Hail Flutie or College Game Day or a team of ninety-plus players flying by chartered jet to a bowl game, who are we to say? We just have to wait and see. And cheer.

Chapter Seven

The Big Break

As hard as he was working to learn and improve, during his first season on the team, Steve operated mostly under the radar. This is not unusual for kickers, who besides the special teams coach, really don't have a kicking coach per se.

"No college in the country has a kicking coach," said Steve. "You're limited in the number of coaches you can have and most teams would rather have someone coaching tight ends or the offensive line. Not kickers! The special teams coaches I had over the years knew some stuff, but for the most part, you have to figure things out on your own. Watch a lot of film and see what you're doing wrong."

Luckily, Steve was used to practicing solo. Still, as a member of the football team, he had the benefit of working with trainers and assistants who were getting to know him well. As far as the head coach (who had yet to catch on to the Sid Vicious thing) was concerned, though, it was good that Steve had learned to speak only when spoken to.

"One time, Coach O'Brien said his name wrong and Steve corrected him," said Johnny Ayers. "Then Coach O'Brien says, 'Yeah. I know. Don't care.'"

Enough said.

"You don't get much of a chance to deal with the head coach when you're the back-up kicker," said Steve. "You deal with your position coach first. There's a hierarchy. I got that."

Steve actually appreciated and admired Coach O'Brien's straight-forward, no-nonsense style.

"I loved him as a coach," said Steve. "I thought he was awesome. He was a very militaristic kind of guy. The discipline was reflected in our play and our practice style but not so much in terms of anything off the field. He was never a micro-manager. There was an expectation that we would do the right thing, that we were all men and could handle ourselves. We could show up to class on our own. He sort of empowered everyone by giving us that type of responsibility."

Author and former Director of Sports Media Relations at BC, Reid Oslin, explained it this way: "O'Brien was a Naval Academy graduate and a former Marine Corps officer," said Oslin. "I think he probably put in place an environment where certain things are expected. Sometimes you don't have to put rules in place. It's understood how you as a player will conduct yourself, whether it's in the classroom or the community or whatever. When you build a program like Tom O'Brien did, these things fall into place."

Being on the football team, even when you're a guy who isn't playing, isn't all about work and responsibility. Especially when you're a kicker.

As Steve Bushee, Assistant AD/Sports Medicine, tells it: "The kickers don't have to go to all the same meetings as the other players in the afternoon so they would all come in – the kickers, punters and long snappers—and jump in the hot whirlpool. It was like the special teams tub club. I used to bust on them. I'd walk by and say, 'Did the waitress come by and take your drink orders?'"

Or, on particularly cold mornings or afternoons, sometimes the kickers, who don't participate in the entire team practice, would temporarily make themselves scarce. When they showed up again, Bushee would say, "Welcome back, gentlemen. How was the hot chocolate?"

Kickers are used to being the punch line of the joke. Often, until they kick the game-winning field goal, they are the Rodney Dangerfields of their teams. No respect.

"Jeremy Trueblood used to head-butt me on this way out of the locker room, to the point where he had to start chasing me," said Johnny Ayers. "And I got hit by as many balls of tape from the linemen as you can imagine. Every day, (offensive tackle) Gosder Cherilus would un-tape his knees, ball up the tape and throw it at me. Some days he'd hit me, some days he'd miss. But I knew every day to expect it."

Steve took Johnny's lead and never took things too seriously. There was never a shortage of laughs, especially in the locker room where some stuff (Vaseline inside a guy's helmet, a cup of water perfectly placed atop a locker so it will fall when a guy opens the door) never seems to get old.

There was plenty of fun to be had during down time, too. Many of the players ate lunch together at one particular table in the cafeteria that was informally known as the football table. At least once a week, Steve and Jamie Silva were joined there by Paul Stark, who worked in the grounds department at BC.

"Paul would just come right in and sit down with us," said Steve. "He was a salt of the earth, blue collar guy; kind of reminded me of home. He had no problem pointing out everything we did wrong to us, but if he heard kids bad-mouthing the football team, he'd jump in and defend us."

The team always ate together after practice, too, piling their plates high at buffets consisting of hearty, comfort food such as steak, prime rib, chicken and potatoes. And the nights before games were mostly relaxing times where the team would have dinner then gather in a room in the team hotel and set up a projector to watch a movie.

Then comes game day. Nothing compares to the thrill a player feels the first time he puts on a uniform and runs through the tunnel and out onto the field for a top-level college football game. Even though he is the number three guy and unlikely to play, it's still a thrill.

Steve's first official game as a member of the team was the Eagles' 2005 home match-up against Florida State. Despite the fact that he spent the game on the sidelines, he was dressed and ready to go, which was incredibly gratifying. Although the uniform itself left something to be desired.

"My first uniform must have belonged to a former tight end," said Steve. "It was so big and it didn't have my name on it. Whoever's name had been on the jersey before had been peeled off; there was still this goo where the letters had been. It looked really bad! It was down to my knees with no name on the back. Not that I needed it at the time but it was a humbling experience."

By the next home game, Steve had been issued a uniform that was closer to his actual size. This one had his name on the back, although the eleven letters in *Aponavicius* were definitely a tight fit. Steve didn't give his uniform much thought, though. If anything, the only piece of equipment he paid attention to was his shoes.

At first, Steve wore a Nike soccer cleat on his left foot and a Reebok football cleat on his right foot. The Nike cleat, which he wore one-size too small so he could feel the impact of the ball, was also colored completely black to conceal the logo. (Reebok sponsored the Eagles).

Because Ryan Ohliger was right-footed, Steve was able to wear some of his left cleats. Later, Steve switched to all Reebok footwear when his Nike cleat wore out and the equipment manager let him know they'd no longer be buying brands other than Reebok.

Even though he had the right shoes, Steve was still only kicking in practice. Although he never booted a ball in live game situations, even on practice days, Steve learned a lot about the precise nature of how to kick.

"If you kick the ball on the wrong part of your foot by an inch, the ball goes wide by three feet instead of going straight," said Steve. "It's unbelievable the precision that goes into it."

Obviously, the kick itself is important. But the set-up of the kick is just as crucial. According to Steve, he quickly found out that you can't underestimate the role of the holders and the snappers.

"When you get a bad snap, it's so much harder to kick," he said. "It's about 1.2 seconds from snap to kick. If you kick the ball in 1.3 or 1.4 seconds, it's going to get blocked. If you kick it in 1.1 seconds, you're probably going to miss it because it's there too early. So, 1.18 or 1.22 is the range you want to be in. Anything under 1.25, you're probably going to get there. But it's such a precise, precise thing. There are lots of moving parts."

The moving parts are people, the kind of athletes that, like Steve, are people who enjoy analyzing and figuring things out for themselves. Then, they put it all together as a functioning group.

"There is an esprit de corps that is created between all those specialists, the snapper, the holder, the guy who kicks field goals, the punter and the long snapper," said Special Teams Coach Jerry Petercuskie. "In order to be very, very good they have to work as one. They have to be on the string. It takes a lot of effort to make sure that the operation goes down without a hitch. It takes a lot of time. They work extremely hard at doing that. It doesn't just happen."

Between practices and home games, Steve had an extremely busy first semester at BC. But due to the fact that NCAA rules only allow for the team to travel sixty of its hundred or so players to road games, when the team played out of town, Steve, and other players did not go along. Those who were not on the travel squad got the day off.

The one exception was the bowl game that year, The MPC Computers Bowl against Boise State. College teams are allowed to travel their entire team to bowl games so for the first time, Steve joined his teammates to hit the road.

Although the team normally traveled together on one plane, this particular year, for some reason they took two smaller planes, one for the traveling squad and one for the forty or so players on the non-traveling squad, which meant that Steve's group had plenty of space to stretch out on the long flight out west.

"I was excited about going, but I remember everybody thinking it was weird that we were going to Boise," said Steve. "We'd had a pretty good year, ending the season 9-3. We were 6-2 or 5-3 in the conference but there were teams that were 3-5 in the conference getting picked over us for bigger bowl games. We had a really good year but weren't rewarded for it."

The reason some selection committees were reluctant to invite Boston College to their bowl games was the school's reputation for not traveling as many fans to games as bigger schools with more alumni, such as Wisconsin, Michigan or Ohio State. There was a good outcome to the bowl in Boise that year, though.

Not only did the Eagles win (27-21), but the ACC changed its rule to state that there has to be a two loss difference for a team to get jumped in bowl game selection.

"That was directly a result of us," said Steve.

The team arrived in Boise on Christmas Eve and the game itself was played a few later. Even though players who weren't in pre-season camp did not get to stand in line for the bowl game player gifts, (up to $500 worth per NCAA rules), Steve had a chance to celebrate with his sister, Lauren, and his brother-in-law, Brian, who joined him in Boise on Christmas Day.

As far as Steve was concerned, there was nothing better than being at a bowl game over Christmas even if it is played on a field of blue turf in crazy weather conditions.

"It was nice weather all week then the day of the game, it was the worst weather I have ever seen," said Steve. "It rained, it snowed, it hailed, and then there was freezing rain. All in the course of one game. It was the first and only time I ever experienced hail with a football helmet on."

It wasn't just the weather that made the game exciting. The Eagles got off to a big lead, then Boise State came storming back. A last minute interception of an attempted touchdown pass that would have won it for Boise State, put BC over the top.

"It might be the last time Boise lost on that blue field," said Steve.

Many people critique the lack of a structured college football playoff at season's end to determine the national championship. But then there are those who ultimately embrace the bowl system. (Especially with at least one rule change that makes it somewhat fairer).

"A lot of people hate the bowl system but I think it's one of the best things about college football that half the teams get to end their year winning a game," said Steve. "End on a high note."

As the season came to a close, Steve had no idea what to expect the following year. He appreciated how far he had come, being reminded of that fact in an especially amusing way when during the team banquet he spotted his painted-up self in the stands at the Army game during a season highlights video.

Steve knew he would be on the team for the 2006 season, and although his prospects were a little brighter with the number-two kicker graduating, he would remain a non-scholarship player.

As far as playing time, his expectations were realistic.

"I was still in shock that I was on the team," Steve said. "My freshman year I never thought I'd play, I never thought I'd travel to a game. I never thought I'd do anything. The next year I still had no expectations regarding whether or not I would play."

During pre-season, no one knew for sure whether or not he would make the roster, but the thing was, Steve's coaches and teammates were starting to expect something from him. They couldn't help but notice how their back-up kicker was evolving.

"When he first came out, he's kicking balls into the backs of linemen," said Johnny Ayers. "But he just kept plugging away. He worked, worked, worked all year long and never said much. He was the nicest, quietest, most down to earth guy. I fell in love with the kid. Then, he started becoming a pretty good kicker. His improvement was starting to show."

"Steve wasn't a very good kicker at first," said Coach Petercuskie. "He was out there and we needed a back-up guy. This kid worked in the weight room, put on weight, kicked the ball, went to camps. He did an outstanding job on his own to get better. He was extremely coachable. He had a great demeanor and he worked really, really hard."

Strength Coach Todd Rice agreed.

"I remember the first time he kicked, the thing kind of died as it went over the crossbar," said Rice. "But everybody needs time to develop and he was one of our most consistent guys and one of ourhardest working guys. It was really endearing and he garnered the respect of his teammates because of it. When he kept improving in the weight room and improving in practice, we all started to think, this guy might kick some day. I told him, 'You know, Sid, you're going to screw up and end up being a place kicker.'"

At the beginning of the 2006 season, Steve was added to the travel squad. He would be traveling with the team to all of the away games, but unless he was otherwise notified, he'd spend the games on the sidelines. Home games, too. For the first few games against Central Michigan, Clemson, BYU, N.C. State, and Maine, that's what he did.

Although, during the season opener against Central Michigan, for a brief time, he thought he was going to play.

"Ohliger (the starter) had gotten hurt earlier in the week," said Steve. "We were up 31-10 and Coach O'Brien came over and said, 'Alright, the next kick is yours.' So, whether it was a field goal or extra point, I was going to go in because we were way ahead and Ohliger was hurt. I was thinking, wow, I better get ready. But then Central Michigan scored two quick touchdowns and Coach O'Brien came back and said, 'You're not kicking.'"

So, Steve stayed on the sidelines. For the time being.

Then came the first week in October. There was no game scheduled for that upcoming Saturday -- the Eagles had a bye week— and BC fans were facing a weekend without football. Even though the fans would be forced to suffer, the players, whose schedules are jam-packed from August to December, couldn't wait for a couple of days off.

Some of the players intended to head home for the weekend. Some planned to study or sleep or do nothing at all. And not surprisingly, some of the players decided to start the weekend early by hitting the town Thursday night.

College guys have been blowing off steam since college guys were invented but this particular night, sometime after midnight, something went wrong inside The Kells, a popular Irish bar and nightclub on Brighton Avenue in Allston. It probably started when somebody said something to somebody else and a friend of that person took offense. Then it escalated, most likely when somebody mouthed off about certain things a football player did or did not do on the field and the player put down his beer and took the bait.

A huge brawl erupted and people inside the bar spilled into the street. The cops were called and although no one was badly hurt, for one participant in particular, the damage was done.

By midday Friday, people started to hear about the fight. Evidently there were several BC football players directly or indirectly involved in the fracas, but only one, kicker Ryan Ohliger, was identified by witnesses.

The story was in the newspapers and even Ohliger himself talked openly about the fight in front of friends and teammates the next day so it was only a matter of time before the coaches caught wind of it. As expected, that afternoon Coach Tom O'Brien suspended Ohliger indefinitely. The big question now was who would kick in the game against ACC-rival Virginia Tech the following Thursday night?

Even though Steve was officially the number-two kicker on the depth chart, it wasn't a given that he would step in for Ohliger. True, he had been practicing consistently and improving steadily and no question, everybody liked the guy and wanted to give him a chance. But he was an unknown quantity, so Coach O'Brien and his assistants had no choice but to seriously consider their options.

There was Billy Flutie, Doug Flutie's nephew and a redshirted freshman who was recruited to play quarterback (and later played wide receiver), but had kicked and punted in high school. If he kicked, the coaches would have to pull his red shirt. A big decision.

There was punter, Johnny Ayers, who was a great athlete with a strong leg but was untested as a place kicker. There was also wide receiver, Brandon Robinson, who when he wasn't receiving, had done a lot of kicking in high school. Someone even mentioned that safety Jamie Silva had punted in high school. Or, Coach O'Brien could call on Steve. Even if he still couldn't say his name.

This would be a tough decision no matter which team BC was scheduled to play but Virginia Tech was ranked No. 22 and the high profile match-up at Alumni Stadium would play out on national TV. It was a Thursday night game – the only college football game in the country being broadcast that night. Not to mention the fact that Tech was known for its ability to block kicks. All eyes would be on the Eagles as well as their kicker.

So the coaches took a day or two and mulled it over. On Saturday, the players ran through a light practice as the coaches combed through the roster again and again. Not one BC player had ever kicked a field goal in a college game. Was their number two guy up to the task?

For his part, Steve tried not to think about it. That sounds like an extremely tall order, but aren't kickers supposed to be able to tune things out?

"I remember thinking, it will be great either way," said Steve. "I'll either play or I'll never play a game in my entire life."

On Sunday, the team practiced as usual. Afterwards, with still with no word from Coach O'Brien regarding the starting kicker, the players went and ate lunch, taking care to sidestep the very large elephant in the room.

Then, that afternoon, just before the special teams meeting, Coach Petercuskie pulled Steve aside and said, "Alright. We're going with you."

The player who people called Sid Vicious couldn't stifle his enormous, goofy grin. "Awesome," he said. "Awesome!"

The next couple of days, the players, coaches and their new, very green, starting kicker did their best to act as if things were business as usual. So as not to call too much attention to the situation or to add to the accumulating pressure, most of his teammates said little or nothing to Steve.

"With kickers, it's such a mental thing that it's best if you just kind of stay away from them," said Johnny Ayers.

According to Jamie Silva, the players didn't have to act detached. They truly believed that Steve could do the job.

"Maybe the coaches were a little worried," he said. "Or Steve himself. But we had confidence in him. The guy had never played football before but obviously he was a good athlete. He played soccer and baseball in high school and we saw how he worked. We knew he could do it."

The media who latched on to the "Superfan Turned Starting Kicker" story that week hadn't been privy to what Steve had been doing for the last year or so.

"He had been working hard for over a year," said Coach Petercuskie, "So, when his opportunity came, he was ready."

His teammates were confident. And his coaches displayed their belief in the novice lefty simply by choosing him to start. Still, Steve had to perform during the game or Thursday night could be his first and last as a starting college football player.

"We thought he was ready," said Coach O'Brien. "But you never really know. You take all those practice kicks and spend all those hours and you try to put yourself in scrimmage situations that are under pressure but you can't ever create the scenario where there are thousands of people in the stands and the band's playing and the lights go on and you know that the TV cameras are on. You just hope the character of this kid and his inner strength comes to the front and allows him to be successful."

Steve came to practice Monday feeling cheerful and upbeat. He had nothing to lose, really, and if he just kept doing what he had been doing all year long, he had no worries.

The team went through their typical drills to complete the first half of practice. Business as usual. Then, as they typically do, the kickers, punters and snappers peeled off by themselves away from the rest of the team for the second half of practice where they play kicking games, run laps or do calisthenics. This particular day, they started playing a little two-on-two, where two-man teams square-off in simulated game situations.

"We would play two-on-two a lot," said Steve. "You've never seen anything more pitiful than a bunch of kickers playing two-on-two. Mostly, we'd play just to pass the time. Johnny Ayers, who was our resident athlete on the K-unit (the kicking unit), would show us all sorts of football moves and scenarios that real players did that we would never get to do."

So, the kickers ran a couple of plays, then Johnny decided to demonstrate how to stiff arm somebody. For the next play, Johnny lined up facing Steve. Then he thrust his arm forward, and hit Steve on the shoulder pad, knocking him backwards.

"I got right up on Steve like a close cornerback and he went to get off the line and I kind of jacked him up," explained Johnny. "Then, he kind of stumbled backwards and stepped in a hole. He immediately dropped to the ground grabbing his ankle. I thought, oh my God, I've just taken out our kicker!"

"For some reason, I was off balance when he hit me," said Steve. "So my whole body spun around while my plant foot stayed in the same place. My ankle just popped! It was the loudest pop I've ever heard. I thought it broke."

The other players just stood there in stunned silence as Steve hobbled back up to his feet.

"I told him, let's get some ice on this right now," said Johnny. "I was having a panic attack. Anxiety was taking over my body. Don't tell me I just took away this kid's life dream!"

Twenty minutes later, Steve was called on to kick during the wrap-up of practice.

"When I went to kick the first ball," he said. "My ankle gave out and I kicked straight into the ground. I figured I probably stretched out a ligament. It was horrible! Everything had been going right and now everything was going wrong."

Steve stopped kicking and slowly limped his way to the training room.

"The coaches were not happy," he said. "I was the only kicker left and I was sitting there on the training table with the fattest ankle you've ever seen. They had to be kicking themselves at that point, like, he hurt himself doing what?"

In order to rest his ankle, Steve didn't kick at all during practice the next day. On Wednesday, he kicked only a few times. Although everyone could see his taped-up ankle, he didn't mention the injury to his teammates.

"The previous year I could have broken my leg and it wouldn't have mattered," he said. "But I finally had a chance to help this team and actually do something. Short of having my legs cut off I was going to play in that game."

Chapter Eight

Thursday Night Lights

As it turned out, Steve didn't have much time to obsess about his injury or Thursday's game. By Tuesday afternoon, the story was out about the kicker who had never played in a football game.

The media was intrigued. People wanted to know, where did this kid come from?

During one of his first pre-game interviews, Steve mentioned that, by the way, before he walked on to the football team last year he was a painted-up Superfan watching the game from the stands. When BC's media relations director, Chris Cameron, dug up video of a bare-chested (minus the maroon and gold paint) Steve wearing a safari hat and cheering wildly for his future teammates from the front row, the story really caught fire.

Stories about the walk-on wonder with the tough-to-pronounce last name ran in *The Boston Herald, The Boston Globe,* BC's student paper, *The Heights,* as well as Pennsylvania papers including *The Easton Express-News* and *The Morning Call.* The Associated Press picked it up. *Sports Illustrated* ran a piece. Even a Lithuanian newspaper ran a story.

Reporters from local radio and TV stations called one after another and a producer from The Ellen DeGeneres Show left a message. Steve was featured on NESN's SportsDesk, Good Morning America, and the ESPN shows Around the Horn and Cold Pizza. His parents were getting dozens of calls at home from friends and family as well as reporters. Producers from ESPN, which would be broadcasting the game Thursday night, wanted to know where the kicker's parents would be sitting so they could interview them and more importantly, film their reaction after Steve's kicks.

According to Kevin Murphy, Steve's roommate and the football team's student equipment manager, activity and traffic in their dorm increased exponentially that week.

"There would be knock after knock on our door," said Murphy. "People were stopping by to wish him good luck and put up posters on our door that said, 'Go Steve!' and "Take down VT!'"

The media relations department was swamped with calls. Kelly Wheeler, Assistant Director for Football Operations, remembers the number one question she got during the days leading up to the game.

"Everybody was asking how to say his name," said Wheeler. "Luckily for me I'd taken it upon myself to learn his name from the start. Everybody just called him Sid Vicious. But now we had to say, AH-pah-NAH-vih-chis."

Incredibly, all the attention didn't seem to rattle Steve.

"He just thought, oh, this is fun and I'm going to enjoy this," said Johnny Ayers. "I don't think he ever took himself too seriously which allowed him to stay relaxed. I think that's the thing that ultimately made Steve so successful. He never really thought too much of it."

Jamie Silva agreed that Steve did a great job of handling the pressure leading up to his debut. Specifically, he remembers encouraging him to savor the moment. "I told him, you're living the dream right now!" he said. "Thirteen months ago you were dressed up, sitting in the stands for a game. You better enjoy this."

According to Steve, he was able to look forward to his first game rather than dread it because he was blissfully unaware. Clueless.

"Looking back, I really wasn't nervous," said Steve. "I was excited. I would have been nervous if I realized at the time what was ultimately at stake. But at that point, I never thought I'd be playing for more than one game."

Basically, he was operating under the premise that he was innocent until proven guilty. He told Mike Blouse, a reporter for his hometown newspaper, *The Express-Times,* "Well, I haven't missed any kicks yet so everyone's behind me for now."

His laid-back attitude served him well but at the same time, his nonchalance almost landed him in the doghouse with his teammates when prior to the game he told reporters, "People have no expectations so I've got nothing to lose."

Quarterback Matt Ryan and other veterans on the team quickly reminded him that four-and-one BC had plenty to lose and this was in fact, the big time.

Without question, the October Twelfth BC-Virginia Tech game was the hottest ticket in town that week. Normally, competition for the attention of Boston sports fans is fierce but as it turned out, the New England Patriots had a bye week, the Red Sox season was over, the Celtics' season hadn't started yet and the Bruins were out of town. No other college football games were on TV that night so BC had the town and the national television audience to itself.

The atmosphere was super-charged on campus that evening, partly because Thursday night games are a rarity. (Boston College has a standing agreement with the town of Newton, Massachusetts, to play only one weeknight game every four years.)

Going in, BC had the better record, (4-1), but the Eagles were still recuperating from their last minute, 17-15 heartbreak loss—their only loss of the season-- to NC State three weeks prior. In fact, both teams had lost one conference game apiece, although the Hokies had not been beaten in a conference road game in two years. Interestingly enough, when it came to Thursday night games on ESPN, the Hokies had an impressive record of 12-1. (Guess who handed them their single Thursday night loss in Blacksburg, Virginia back in 1995? The Boston College Eagles).

Stats and factoids aside, both teams needed and badly wanted this win.

Game night finally arrived. Less than an hour before kick-off, as the crowd (including Heisman Trophy winner Doug Flutie) filed into a lit-up Alumni Stadium, the BC Eagles finished their pre-game preparations in the locker room. As Steve checked the tape on his right ankle, safety Jamie Silva walked over, slapped the kicker on the shoulder and offered a last minute piece of advice.

"You've been kicking for a year and you nail these things all the time," he said. "Just go out there and pretend that it's practice."

Steve, who had been all smiles since he woke up that morning, nodded in agreement. "Sounds like a plan," he said.

Out on the field, the excitement was building and the topic of many pre-game conversations involved Steve Aponavicius. BC Defensive Coordinator, Bill McGovern, remembered one such conversation.

"Before the game, one of the Virginia Tech coaches came up to me and said, 'What's the deal with your kicker? He came out of the stands?' Tech's kicker was around 270 pounds! Plus, with their reputation for blocking kicks, they were probably salivating."

The ESPN broadcast team had plenty to say about BC's new kicker as well. Leading up to the official start, announcer Kirk Herbstreit talked over a shot of screaming, gold-t-shirt wearing BC Superfans saying, "The students are getting pumped up. But from their ranks, just a year ago, he's become a central player in tonight's game…"

Then, sideline reporter Erin Andrews took over. "This is a script right from the movies," she said. "It's BC's version of Rudy. Steve Aponavicius. What a difference a year makes. A year ago he was in the cheering section, his body all painted-up…"

As a video segment of Steve during his brush with Superfandom flashed onto the screen, Andrews continued, "There he is wearing a 'B' on his chest. Tonight, he's kicking for the Eagles…"

As the piece went on, "…He's even got his very own nickname, Sid Vicious…" the Eagles and their kicker, who stood a head shorter than most of his teammates, ran out on the field to the sound of thundering applause.

After a last minute warm-up and a few words from the position coaches, the Eagles clustered together on their sideline as their opponents did the same across the field. Then the captains from each side walked to the fifty-yard line where the referee made the toss. BC won it and deferred. So the Eagles would kick-off. Steve would kick-off.

Then, in the first play of the game, his first play as a football player, Steve took the ball from the official, placed it on the tee, and walked backwards a couple of yards. Then, as he'd done in practice dozens and dozens of times, he took a few running steps forward, connected with the ball and booted it some sixty-two yards all the way to Virginia Tech's three-yard line.

The ESPN announcers kept the narrative moving. "Not bad…Now he's a college football player…"

Steve ran downfield in pursuit of the Hokie receiver ("Look!" said Herbstreit, "He wants to make a tackle!") but his teammates beat him to it; the receiver was already down.

As the kick-off unit jogged off the field, the people in the stadium crowd, most of them on their feet, cheered enthusiastically. But the noise made by the capacity crowd of some 44,500 fans paled in comparison to the whoop let out some three hundred miles away by a group of thirty or so people gathered in a house in the College Hill neighborhood of Easton, Pennsylvania.

"Most of the city of Easton was over at our house to watch the game on TV," said Ian McCutcheon. "Basically my mom invited everyone in the whole town who had any connection to Steve to come over."

The McCutcheon's home was the ideal place to gather. Not only was it centrally located on Easton's Lafayette Street, but also they had four TV's.

So, that evening the McCutcheons dragged every chair in the house into the living room and a couple dozen longtime friends of friends of friends, parents of friends, children of friends and grandparents of friends piled into the their home. Steve's former baseball and soccer teammates jockeyed for position, sitting on coolers, on the floor or in chairs in front of the big screen TV with their former coaches, all Pennsylvanians who suddenly had a stake in the outcome of a game featuring teams from Virginia and Massachusetts.

The anticipation had been building for days, especially among Steve's closest friends who began emailing and calling each other the moment they heard the news of Ryan Ohliger's suspension. By game time, the adrenaline in the room had peaked.

"Every time there would be a close-up or a shot of Steve, there'd be this big round of applause in the room," said Ian. "It was hilarious because the year before we were watching BC play Boise State in the bowl game. Steve was there on the sidelines and we were just hoping to see him in a background shot. Now, he was front and center. It was crazy!"

As BC prepared to kick-off, the surge of energy in the McCutcheon house evaporated into a hush.

"Everybody was nervous," said Ian. "My heart was racing. There was a mild sense of dread because Steve had never done this before. It's not like we'd seen Steve play high school football for four years and knew what he could do. It was as much a mystery to us as it was to anyone else."

After the successful kickoff, the first quarter proceeded with neither team scoring. Then, as the clock ran down, suddenly, the broadcasters boomed, "Fumble!" and all eyes turned towards the nearest TV to see BC receiver cornerback DeJuan Tribble scoop up the ball dropped by Virginia Tech receiver David Clowney at the Hokies' twenty-four-yard line. Cheers filled the house as the TV cameras trained on Steve, who was taking warm-up kicks into the sideline net.

Then the BC offense stalled. On fourth down, Coach O'Brien opted to go for the touchdown instead of a field goal (which would have been a long one, forty-three yards for Steve's first-ever attempt), and the Eagles lost the ball. No kick yet.

Then, late in the first half, BC broke the scoreless tie when quarterback Matt Ryan connected with wide receiver, Kevin Challenger, for a crisp, fifteen-yard touchdown pass. "OK, he's up!" "Here he comes!"

As Steve jogged onto the field and the net behind the goal posts was raised, partygoers in Easton put down their sodas or their beers and their paper plates stacked with hot dogs and held their collective breath.

"Shhhhhhhhhhhhhhhhhh!"

The snap. The hold. The steps leading up to the kick…

Then, just before he made contact with the ball, a shriek came from the kitchen.

"He did it!" yelled Ian's mom, Pat McCutcheon. "He did it!"

Then, a second or two later, the group gathered around the living room TV watched their guy kick the ball through the uprights.

"It's good!"

After the high-fives, hugs and cheers died down, Ian's dad, Bruce, went into the kitchen to investigate what appeared to be his wife's recently acquired psychic abilities. It didn't take long to figure out that the kitchen TV, which was connected directly to the cable wire as opposed to a cable box, was getting the signal a full three seconds before the TV in the living room.

For the rest of the night, a spot in the McCutcheons' kitchen near the tiny, fourteen-inch TV mounted on a shelf next to the refrigerator became as coveted as a seat in a fifty-yard-line luxury box.

After Steve's successful kick, the cameras flashed to Ben and Jan in the stands, hugging and slapping high-fives with the other football parents. They had no way to know they were on TV so people at the party took turns calling them to update them.

"Call the A's," said Pat. "They're on again!"

Jan tried to answer the phone but it was impossible to hear over the crowd so she stopped picking up. Besides, as Ben said later, "I didn't want to use up my minutes."

Everyone watching the game in Easton agreed that the extra point was the ideal way for Steve to ease into his role as starting kicker.

"My dad was the first to say that he was really glad Steve's first kick was an extra point," said Ian. "That way he could get on the field and break the ice without having to kick a thirty-something-yard field goal.
From a calm-your-nerves standpoint, that was the best scenario."

Halftime came and went. Then, well into the third quarter, the Eagles were up 7-3 when Hokie quarterback Sean Glennon fumbled, or so it appeared. Virginia Tech Head Coach Frank Beamer asked for a review of the play, which was ruled an incomplete pass. No fumble.

The Hokies got the ball back, but on the very next play, Eagles linebacker Jo-Lonn Dunbar intercepted Glennon's pass. BC got the ball back with even better field position than if the fumble had stood.

After another couple of plays, the Eagles' drive stopped short. At fourth down and more than a yard, Coach O'Brien decided to go for a field goal. Steve was already on the field; all he needed was a nod from his coach. When he got it he jogged—ran, really-- into position as Herbstreit asked the question on everyone's minds, "Can the lefty convert?"

Then, with 9:11 left to play in the third quarter, long snapper Jack Geiser snapped the ball to holder Chris Crane who set the ball down softly. Then, Steve booted the ball and from thirty-six yards out, it sailed directly through the uprights.

Again, it was Herbstreit, who exclaimed, "How 'bout that?" His partner, Chris Fowler added, "Steve Aponavicius, the walk-on. Welcome to college football!"

"After that field goal, the place went crazy," said Todd Rice, who was watching with the team from BC's side of the field. "It was almost as if the fans sensed something from us on the sidelines that something really special just happened."

Some seventy miles away from Easton in Paoli, Pennsylvania, Steve's sister, Kristin, and her husband, Jamie, choked back tears watching Steve's teammates hug him and lift him in the air as if he'd just won a championship game for the Eagles.

They celebrated in Seattle where Steve's sister, Lauren, and her husband, Brian, had left their offices early and been glued to their TV since the game began. In fact, because their regular cable TV provider wouldn't be broadcasting the game, Brian made it a point to order DirectTV earlier in the week, just so they could see the game. Aunts, uncles and cousins in other parts of Pennsylvania and Massachusetts were also watching ESPN that night.

In other parts of Easton they were watching, too.

Although Steve never played football for Easton High School, Head Coach Steve Shiffert, the school's winningest coach of all time, was watching. "I wouldn't have missed it," he said. "I got chills as soon as they did that special on Steve right at the start."

Mike Blouse of *The Express-Times,* was also watching even though it was technically his night off. "I'd followed his story from the start," said Blouse. "That was a great night. Every time Steve did anything on the field they retold his story. It was kind of surreal."

Back at the McCutcheon's house, the tears and hugs and elbowing in front of the kitchen TV continued.

"My mom cried twice after Steve made his first field goal," said Ian. "The rest of the game we were all hoping BC would win but we didn't want them to score a touchdown. We wanted them to get down to the ten or fifteen-yard line, and then stop. We wanted as much Steve time as possible."

The Easton crowd would get their wish. Not long after his first three-pointer, which put the Eagles up 10-3, BC was yet again in field goal range.

"It was the only game where I heard people cheer when we didn't get it (a first down) on fourth down and had to kick a field goal," said Steve. "That never happened before and won't happen again."

Once again, Steve made a perfect kick, this time a twenty-yarder from the right hash. The score was 13-3.

Following more excellent play by the Eagles' defense, which continued to frustrate the Hokie offense, BC did in fact score another touchdown, when in the fourth quarter Matt Ryan again connected with Kevin Challenger, and Steve, by this time looking like an old pro, tacked on the extra point.

Before the game's end, the Eagles scored another two points on the Hokies' fourth-and-seventeen when the snap sailed through punter Nic Schmitt's hands and through the back of the endzone for a safety.

Final score: BC: 22, Virginia Tech: 3.

After the final seconds ticked away, the victorious Eagles ran onto the field. Reporters clustered around Steve who graciously talked to each one. When he finished the interviews, he sprinted to where a cluster of his teammates were standing in front of the Superfans in the stands. The players waved and held their helmets in the air as the students cheered and roared. When they saw Steve, they roared even louder.

"They were just so proud of him," said Steve Bushee. "It was one of their own making the leap out of the stands and onto the field. It was a big deal for those fans."

Then Steve spotted Bill Lytch, the student who joined him in painting-up at the first Boston College home game the previous year. (Steve was the "B" and Lytch was the "C"). When he saw Lytch, Steve took a running start and leapt into the stands. The Superfans grabbed Steve and held onto him as he dangled in the air. They chanted and cheered until they were hoarse. The Rover Nation themselves couldn't have done it any better.

A couple of hours before BC's triumphant win that night, just a few miles from the McCutcheon's party on College Hill, Steve's aunt, Milda Scrima, was busy tidying up her mother's home. That morning, Filomena Aponavicius, (Milda's mother and Steve's grandmother), had been released from the hospital after checking in a few days prior with severe back pain, elevated blood pressure, dizziness and other unsettling symptoms.

After diagnosing a diseased aorta and deciding that surgery would be too dangerous for Filomena, the doctors released her and then Milda and Steve's mother, Jan, brought her home.

Despite the fact that she'd just turned 90, the problem with her aorta was the first serious illness Filomena had suffered in many years. She never smoked and didn't drink much. Incredibly, she took no regular medication, partly because she didn't need it, and partly because she said the side effects were worse than the medicine. So why bother?

For the most part, she didn't like going to doctors; she said they talked way too fast and because her English wasn't the best, it was difficult to understand them.

Luckily, her health was so good that she hadn't needed to see the doctor very often. Filomena still lived on her own and although she didn't drive, she could walk up and down the steps and take care of things around the house. Of course her family helped out – both Milda and her husband, Don, as well as Ben and Jan, lived close by and between them, someone managed to stop by every day to check on her.

Steve's aunt, Ruta Koslov, lived about an hour-plus drive away in

Harleysville, Pennsylvania, and between nephews and nieces and other friends, Filomena had plenty of company.

That evening, as Milda cleaned up and put groceries away, her mother lay upstairs resting in her bedroom. After she got things in order, Milda walked upstairs and checked on Filomena, then she came back down and flopped on the living room couch.

The last few days had been hectic. Between worrying about her mother, staying up with her and getting her home from the hospital early that morning, Milda hadn't gotten much sleep. She fought the urge to nod off, though. It was an exciting night for the Aponavicius family – her nephew was playing in his first college football game – and she wanted to stay up and hear the reports from the game.

Filomena had cable TV but her package didn't include ESPN, so at one point in the afternoon, Milda went home, turned on her two TV's and set up the VCR's to record the game. She figured it was best to set up both TV's in case something went wrong with one of them.

Normally, her husband, Don, would have taped the game for her – certainly he would never miss such a big event—but he was traveling on business. So Milda set things up, left the TV's on in her empty house and went back to be with her mother.

Jan and Ben had left Easton that morning in order to make it to Boston in time for the 7:30 PM kickoff. In fact, Ben had stopped by his mother's house briefly before they left town, but when he saw that Milda was out picking up prescriptions, he didn't want to knock on the door and wake up his mother. So he headed home to pick up Jan and they started off on their six-hour drive.

Just before the game began, Milda got several phone calls alerting her that the ESPN announcers were doing a pre-game piece about Steve. Her daughter, Lisa, was one of the first to check-in.

"Mom!" she said. "Steve's on TV! They're talking about him and – oh! They just zoomed in on Uncle Ben and Aunt Jan!"

Milda ran upstairs to give her mother the news.

"Mother, Steven's on TV!" she said. "And Ben and Janice…"

"Wonderful!" said Filomena.

And Milda went back downstairs. Soon she got another call.

"He's about to kick a field goal…."

Again she walked up a flight to tell her mother the news.

"Steven's kicking….a field goal, I think…"

But he didn't kick.

"Never mind. The other team got the ball back."

Soon, the phone rang again. Thankfully, Milda was still in

her mother's room.

"O.K., he's not kicking yet but they just showed him warming up! You can see his face. He's smiling! He doesn't even look nervous."

A bit of time passed without a call so Milda, figuring it was halftime, went back downstairs. Then, just as she stretched out on the living room couch, Lisa called again. Boston College had scored and Steve was about to attempt his first kick as a college football player. Before Milda, (still holding the phone to her ear), could make it up the stairs, Lisa said, "He did it! It's good!"

This time Milda simply called up to her mother.

"Mother he made it!"

"Oh, that's good!" said Filomena.

As the game went on, Milda kept calling upstairs every time there was a development.

"He just made a field goal! They're showing Ben and Janice again!"

At some point, Filomena stopped answering back. She must have gone to sleep, Milda thought. But Milda couldn't help herself. She kept sending up the reports until she dozed off on the couch. Then, she woke up when Lisa called one last time.

"That's it! They won! He's jumping in the stands…"

Finally, Milda went to sleep, too.

Several hours later – it was probably 3:00 AM – Milda woke up and realized, groggily, that she should wake her mother so she could take her medication. She walked upstairs and touched Filomena gently on her shoulder. But Filomena didn't wake. Milda then realized that sometime in the night or the early morning, she wasn't sure which, her mother had died peacefully in her sleep.

Sid Vicious going solo at Alumni Stadium.
Photos by Ronald C. Modra

Ready for his close-up.

Ready, willing and able.

Superfans (minus one).

(L to R): Brother-in-law Jamie,
Jamie Silva and Steve.

Thursday Night Lights:
BC vs. Virginia Tech.
2006
(Aponavicius goes four-for-four).
Photos (center and bottom) courtesy
John Quackenbos, BC Media Relations

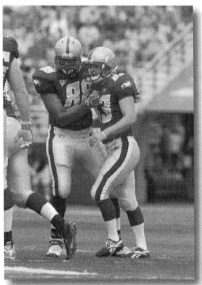

Final score:
BC: 22
VA Tech: 3

Coming full circle: Celebrating with Superfans.
2006

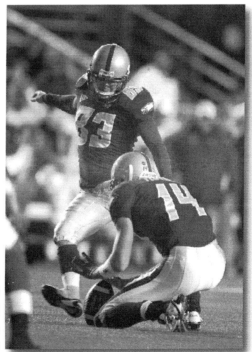

Kicking against Maryland.
2008
Photos (top and bottom)
courtesy John Quackenbos,
BC Media Relations

(L to R): Steve's cousin Lisa Goldizen, her husband, Darrell Goldizen,
his sister Lauren and brother-in-law Brian cheering on BC vs. NC State.

Cheering Section: Meineke Bowl. 2006

Steve celebrates with game MVP Jo-Lonn Dunbar following
BC's win over Navy. Photo: Todd Sumlin / The Charlotte Observer

It's good!
Photo: Jason Miczek

Steve and Taylor.

Chapter Nine

The Starter

As the last of the jubilant crowd filed out of Alumni Stadium, the Eagles players were in their locker room blasting *Thriller,* one of the songs they always played after winning a big game. They were laughing, celebrating, and everybody was clapping Steve on the back and hitting him with towels as they hit the showers.

Under Coach O'Brien's rules, the members of the football team wore suits and ties to home games. The players weren't required to wear suits after the game, so most of his teammates changed into track suits or sweats before heading home. But Steve, who was due at his first post-game press conference, changed back into his suit (a hand-me-down from his brother-in-law, Brian, that was just a little bit too short in the sleeves) before meeting the media in the press room.

"I got a lot of grief for that," said Steve. "But I wanted to look good."

According to Steve Conroy, who attended the press conference for *The Boston Herald,* the rookie kicker seemed at ease as he fielded questions from the press.

"There were a couple of other players with him and they were just watching him in awe," said Conroy. "A year before, this kid was in the stands and here he was handling himself with aplomb in the press conference. It was a sight to see."

Before the game, Steve had his teammates, his coaches, reporters and the fans on his side. He had never missed a field goal in his life, but then again, he'd never made one either. After the game, he still hadn't missed one.

"He hit all his kicks that night," said Conroy. "It was just the perfect story."

The win did more than thrill friends and fans of the unlikeliest of starting kickers. It also propelled the now 5-1 Boston Eagles to their highest ranking of the season (USA Today: No. 25, AP: No. 26). The impressive performance where BC's defense forced four turnovers and held the Hokies to just twenty-one yards in the second half resulted in intangibles such as a shot at a better bowl game bid and a boost in recruiting.

But in the end, the day belonged to Steve Aponavicius.

"Steve outscored the entire Virginia Tech team by himself," said Boston College Athletic Director Gene DeFilippo. "They were ranked No. 22 in the nation at the time and we came in and played them and beat them before a sell-out crowd at home. And they scored no touchdowns. So Steve outscored them all by himself when the year before, he was in the stands cheering."

Upon closer examination, the win, and specifically the successful kicks were even more impressive, considering they came against the Hokies, a team known for blocking kicks.

"Virginia Tech prides itself on special teams play," said Reid Oslin. "They are the acknowledged masters. Their head coach, Frank Beamer, coaches special teams himself. They specifically recruit players who can block kicks. I don't know of any team in college football that has blocked as many kicks as Virginia Tech. So for a rookie kicker to come in, look at all those maroon helmets two feet in front of him, and do what he did? It's remarkable."

Following the game, several of Steve's coaches commented on his storybook night.

"At that game, it wasn't like he had time to warm-up and grow into it," said Defensive Coordinator Bill McGovern. "It was like, boom, here's the fire!"

A lot of guys can do it in practice but in front of 40 or 50,000 people and a TV audience, that's a different ballgame," said Coach Petercuskie. "That takes a special guy."

Perhaps more than anyone else, the boss was breathing a sigh of relief.

"He's really a confident kid," Coach O'Brien said. "Everybody kept asking, what's he going to do? And the kid isn't fazed by anything. The kid had one hell of a time out there. He had more fun than anybody. I'm just glad for the lift he gave us."

According to his teammates, they never had a doubt about how things would turn out.

"Everybody supported him," strong safety Ryan Glasper told The Boston Globe. "We believed in his ability, we watched him kick, and, I mean, he came out this week and I don't think he missed in practice.
So we had confidence in him and I think that helped him out. I told him, 'You got nothing to lose; you got everything to gain from here on out.' I think he took that to heart and just went out and did his job."

"We were just so pumped," said Jamie Silva. "He went four-for-four. But we knew he could do it."

The press conference wrapped-up with a final question from a reporter, "So, Steve, are you going to go to class tomorrow?"

Steve just shrugged. "Yeah, of course. You have to go to class."

The next morning, Steve figured he'd be facing just another ordinary Friday, but when he walked into his 10:00 AM Financial Accounting class, the other forty or so students got up from their seats and gave him a loud standing ovation. He just smiled, blushed a little bit, sat down and opened up his notebook.

Later that week and during the next couple of weeks, students whom he had never met would smile and wave at him and say, "Hi Steve!" "Way to go, Steve!"

"It's unbelievable to think that two weeks ago no one had any idea who I was," he said. "I could have walked around campus naked and nobody would have noticed me."

A lot of kids approached him to say hi and talk about the Virginia Tech game, but it seemed that just as many kept their distance, as if they were somehow intimidated to talk to him. For instance, at parties or in the dining hall, Steve would notice people staring, pointing in his direction or even sometimes, to his amazement, snapping his picture.

"It was so weird," he said laughing. "I couldn't imagine why anyone would want to do that. But it was cool."

In a sign of the times, when Steve logged onto his computer that week, he found himself with three hundred emails in his in box as well as several hundred Facebook friend requests, which were much more welcome than the dozens and dozens of Facebook pokes he received the previous week from Virginia Tech fans ("You're gonna miss! You s#*@!" "We're gonna crush you!")

"I think they were trying to crash my Facebook account," Steve said.

Is there such a term as "cyber-trash talk"?

Over the next few days, Steve continued to ride quite a high, when among other things, he was named ACC Rookie of the Week. A BC Gridiron Club email blast made note of the honor, even though they listed him as Steve *Ponovicius* (sic).

Despite the misspelling, at least the announcement found him in good company. The other ACC players of the week were Josh Beekman, (offensive line), and Jo-Lonn Dunbar (defensive line), both tremendous players who went on to NFL careers.

Soon enough, it was back to business and practice as usual. With one slight change. According to Jamie Silva: "Every day after practice, right when the final whistle would blow and we'd be walking off the field, you'd see about thirty kids run out on the field as if they were trying to impress the coach doing diving passes with their buddies. It was hilarious! We said, 'Steve. Look what you started.'"

As much as his fellow students sought to become the next discovery, the next Sid Vicious, Steve attempted to keep things low key.

"He came in on Sunday after that first game and everybody was happy for him, but it was right back to business," said Todd Rice. "He didn't go around saying I'm the man, skipping workouts. Nothing like that."

Steve's parents, who attended every game from there on out, were excited and proud of their son. Still, they helped keep him grounded through all the hoopla.

"I'd talk to my mom on the phone and the first thing she would say was, 'Did you do your homework yet? How are your grades?'" Steve said. "She didn't want to talk about football. I had to get good grades. I didn't have a choice."

To Steve's way of thinking, this was hardly the time to slack off in the classroom or during football practice. The exact opposite was true. Despite his successful on-field debut, Steve was in suspense regarding his place on the roster. He had no idea whether or not he would get a chance for a command performance.

According to reporter Mike Blouse, "He knew that could have been it for him. He might have just had his fifteen minutes of fame."

Just a few days later, Steve found out where he stood when Coach O'Brien announced that Ohliger would be reinstated for the Florida State game the following week. There was a caveat, though. Ohliger would be performing kick-off duties only. He was listed as back-up place kicker for field goals and PAT's. The starting place-kicker was Steve Aponavicius.

It's safe to say that it stung just a little not to be slated for kickoffs. No doubt part of the reason was that two of his three previous week's kickoffs reached only as far as between the opposing team's ten and twenty-yard lines. The other part, from the coach's point of view, was what to do with Ohliger. Regardless, Steve embraced this incredible opportunity and like the rest of his team, put his mind towards beating Florida State at Doak Campbell Stadium in Tallahassee the following week.

The setting was a thriller, with some 80,000 fans cheering Bobby Bowden's Seminoles, who wore black uniforms for the first time that day to honor the Seminole tribe in Florida. Despite the Seminoles' home field advantage and worries about Eagles quarterback Matt Ryan's injured left foot, BC came out on top, beating their ACC rivals (24-19).

Ryan completed sixteen of twenty-six passes for 262 yards and the Eagles defense held Florida State to just twenty-eight yards rushing. For his part, Steve kept his unblemished record intact when he successfully completed all of his kicks (three PAT's and a third quarter, twenty-six-yard field goal).

Next, the Eagles played Buffalo at home, a BC win (41-0) that provided little drama and again, a perfect day for their new place-kicker.

Inevitably, a kicker is going to miss a few and for Steve, his first-ever miss came against Wake Forest in early November when a forty-yard attempt went wide left.

"It was a really, really cold night game," Steve said. "I remember we had trouble keeping the balls inflated because it was so cold. I remember Matt Ryan was complaining that the ball was flat. There wasn't a lot of juice in the ball that day."

Steve also sustained a particularly grisly injury during that game when following a kickoff, an opposing player's helmet collided with his facemask and he bit completely through his tongue.

"I was spitting blood the entire game," said Steve. "But it was my fault. I never wore a mouth piece which is pretty stupid."

Despite Matt Ryan's career high forty of fifty-seven passes for 402 yards and a touchdown, the Eagles' many mistakes, including two interceptions and a total of ten penalties, gave the Demon Decons the edge and Wake Forest won the game 21-14.

Steve and his teammates offered no excuses.

"I learned fast that you have to put failure behind you," said Steve. "Especially when it comes to kicking, it's do or die. You make it or you miss it."

Steve came to this conclusion partly on his own and partly from advice shared by his teammates and coaches, including Coach O'Brien.

"As a kicker, you have to have a short memory," said O'Brien. "You have to have a lot of confidence in your ability and you have to be able to go from one to the next and not be hung up on what just happened. You have to focus on what's next or when am I going to get my opportunity again."

As unexpected as it might seem, Steve frequently received advice from kickers on opposing teams. Wake Forest kicker Sam Swank was one such player.

The year Steve and Swank met, Swank, who went on to join the roster of three NFL teams and played for the Hartford Colonials of the United Football League in 2010, was the nation's active career leader with sixty field goals. At the time he also held his school record with over one hundred consecutive PAT's and would end the season as Wake Forest's all time leading scorer (337 points).

"Before every game the kickers are out there warming up before everybody else and usually we end up talking to each other a little bit," said

Steve. "You can tell the guys who don't want to talk; they kind of stay away from you. But Swank made it a point to talk to me and share some of his philosophies. It was really cool. You had to listen to a guy like him. He was the best in the ACC for a while."

The Eagles made up for the sting of the Wake Forest loss with two home wins in a row, against Duke (28-7) and Maryland (38-16). The Eagles came into the Maryland game ranked No. 20 and beat the No. 21-ranked Terrapins with a defensive barrage where among other things, Jo-Lonn Dunbar became only the fourth player in NCAA history to return two fumbles for touchdowns in the same game.

The 17-14 loss to Miami during the last game of the regular season meant that despite their 9-3 overall record, the Eagles (5-3 in the conference) would miss the chance to play for the ACC Championship. Even so, from Steve's perspective it was impossible to put a damper on the previous few months.

"That whole year was just fun," Steve said. "I can't think of a better word to describe it. We were winning games. We were on TV almost every week. It was unbelievable."

And it wasn't quite over yet.

At season's end, Boston College was invited to play the U.S. Naval Academy on December 30th at The 2006 Meineke Car Care Bowl in Charlotte, North Carolina. This marked BC's eighth straight bowl game appearance. If the Eagles won, they would count their seventh straight bowl game victory, which was the longest active streak in the country. The team would also finish with ten season wins for only the third time in school history.

BC's Head Coach Tom O'Brien was a 1971 Naval Academy graduate but as it turned out, he would not coach his team against his alma mater. Just a few weeks prior to the game, Boston College Director of Athletics Gene DeFilippo announced that O'Brien had accepted a position as head coach at North Carolina State and would begin his duties there immediately.

The players were universally sorry to see Coach O'Brien go.

"His time at BC was such a good era," said Steve. "He came in following a gambling scandal. The program was in shambles and he was able to turn it around. I think he was very, very underappreciated. Every time we stepped on the field, athletically, we were outmatched. But we were just smarter than everybody else. I think that was a direct result of coaching. Guys like him win in the end."

With Defensive Coordinator Frank Spaziani appointed interim head coach, Eagles players did their best to focus on the matter at hand. The team had confidence in their temporary leader, a long-time protégé of Coach O'Brien's who had ten seasons under his belt with BC, including eight seasons as BC's defensive coordinator, as well as other impressive resume entries that included playing and serving as a graduate assistant to Penn State Head Coach, Joe Paterno. More recently, Spaziani spent nine years on the coaching staff at The University of Virginia and five seasons in the Canadian Football League (two with Winnipeg, three with Calgary). Plus, from 1975-1982, he worked as an offensive assistant at The U.S. Naval Academy. In sum, Spaziani had worked with Coach O'Brien for some thirty years.

Leading up to the bowl game, Coach "Spaz" as his players called him, did his best to instill confidence in his team and the fans.

"We have a system that's been in place here and a staff that's been together for quite a while," said Coach Spaziani, "So we kind of know how to do things, and we have a way of doing it. It's called the BC way."

During pre-game interviews, Coach Spaz once again reiterated that he would not be reinventing the Eagles' wheel.

"There haven't been any program-altering decisions that have been made," he said. "We're trying to take care of this game. Basically what I'm deciding is chocolate or vanilla. Go or stop."

The atmosphere in Charlotte leading up to the game was festive and upbeat with Meineke spokesperson George Foreman and several thousand fans showing up for the Uptown Street Festival and Pep Rally near Bank of America Stadium, the venue where the NFL's Carolina Panthers play. The Aponavicius family was there, along with a hefty contingent of folks from Easton, Pennsylvania, including the Mulrine family, whose friends owned a bar not far from the stadium, providing an ideal gathering spot.

When game day arrived, nearly forty of Steve's family and friends filed into the stadium with over 60,000 other fans and took their seats, mostly in two adjacent rows. Inspired by the days when Steve and his friends led the Rover Nation, Brandon's sister, Katie Mulrine, passed out large poster board letters spelling out A-P-O-N-A-V-I-C-I-U-S.

The Eagles won the coin toss and elected to receive. As soon as both teams took the field for the kick-off, it was obvious that with the possible exception of their kicker and one or to others, to a man, the BC players were bigger than the Midshipmen. So the Eagles had that advantage.

"It looked like the BC guys were a foot taller than the Navy guys," said Steve's brother-in-law, Brian Reidy. "The Navy guys have to be short enough to serve on a nuclear sub, I think."

Despite playing under an interim coach and despite the just-revealed fact that quarterback Matt Ryan had been playing with a broken bone in his left foot for the last seven games and had been wearing a walking boot off-field for at least two months, BC was still favored to win that day.

Everything seemed on track when early in the first quarter, following a drive that lasted only five plays, Matt Ryan ran it in for the first BC touchdown. The Eagles made that one look easy.

Next, Steve stepped up to kick the extra point, which by his eighth game had become a routine chore. A workaday task. But this time, things went awry.

"I kicked it horribly," Steve said. "It hit wide left."

As TV announcer Pam Oliver noted, this was the kicker's first missed extra point of the season. (She also mispronounced his name).

According to Ian McCutcheon, who was in the stands, this was a "your heart sinks" moment.

"That was the worst thing that could have happened because to football fans, extra points are automatic," said Ian. "And that's not true. He'd been perfect on extra points all year. My biggest fear was that this would come back to haunt him."

The Eagles didn't let the missed PAT get them down. It was early in the game. Easy enough for Steve and his teammates to shake it off and close the gap.

"It didn't look like (the miss) was going to be a problem," said Steve. "It still looked like we were going to steam roll them."

But, the plot thickened. Navy was confusing BC defenders with their triple-option offense. At times it seemed as though the Midshipmen were pulling every play out of their playbook, even switching quarterback Kaipo-Noa Kaheaku-Enhada, (a.k.a. "The Flyin' Hawaiian") to another position for one play.

Soon, the Midshipmen scored a touchdown and followed-up by completing the PAT, taking a 7-6 lead. Then, with just over two minutes remaining on the first quarter clock, Navy intercepted the ball. Soon into the second quarter, Navy scored again and the game stood at 14-6.

After another series or two, as the announcers interviewed none other than former BC Coach Tom O'Brien, the Eagles scored and this time, Steve knocked in the PAT. Navy: 14-Boston College: 13.

Then, Navy scored again.

BC got the ball back and quickly moved it downfield seventy-one yards. Then, with just one second left on the clock, despite the distractions of the Navy band members and their goat mascot waving their arms just behind the end zone, Steve booted a twenty-six-yard field goal. It was good.

At half-time, the score was 21-16.

In the locker room, Coach Spaziani, who stood stoically on the sidelines during the first half with his arms folded in front of him, had little to say. "You decide how you want to finish this…"

After half-time, the two teams hit the field again. As George Foreman was being interviewed in the announcer's booth, ("I used to play football when I was younger, but it hurt too much," he said), Navy kicked a field goal, bringing the score to 24-16.

Things were lively after that. First down BC. Interception Navy. BC stops the drive. Matt Ryan sacked. BC fails to score and punts. It's a good one, and soon, BC gets the ball back with good field position. Then, a twenty-five-yard Matt Ryan pass to tight end Ryan Purvis. Touchdown BC!

After the score, the Eagles, down by two, decided to forgo the extra-point kick and attempt a two-point conversion in order to tie the game. But the pass to Tony Gonzalez was incomplete.

"It was a really tough catch," said Steve. "But still, he dropped the ball. Tony came up to me and said, 'Man, I'm so sorry.' And I'm thinking, I'm the one who screwed it up. But he felt bad because it looked like we were going to lose."

Indeed, things didn't look good. Navy had the ball and they were letting the play clock run down. With just over two minutes left, BC called their last time-out as the Navy band played and TV cameras showed Navy fans holding up signs, "We're #1" and "ESPN: Every Sailor Picks Navy," and beginning to celebrate.

The broadcasters, who began to thank the crew, the statisticians, and read the credits, were effectively telling their 6.5 million TV viewers that the game was over. "They're feeling it in Annapolis right now…"

But it wasn't over. Not yet. The clock started and stopped again. The players were jumpy. Offsides, BC. Holding, Navy. Then, a play got underway and incredibly, Navy fumbled and Eagles team captain, Jo-Lonn Dunbar, who had already notched fifteen tackles that day, picked up the ball. BC recovered the fumble!

The celebration among the Navy faithful sputtered to a halt and was replaced by jubilation amongst the BC fans. Then, the stadium became quiet as Matt Ryan stepped back and completed a crisp pass to Ryan Purvis for a first down. Next, BC ran two quick running plays, each for short gains. On the last play, the ball was spotted at mid-field and it suddenly became obvious that the Eagles, who were down by only two points, were setting the stage for a field goal attempt.

Although he dutifully did what his coach had asked, Matt Ryan was very unhappy about the decision not to go for a touchdown pass.

"On the film afterwards, you could see how visibly upset he was," said Steve. "It's understandable. He's a competitor and it was frustrating. He wanted to win more than anybody."

With just three seconds remaining on the clock, the kicking unit hit the field. In the stands, many BC fans were linked together arm-in-arm trying to lower their collective heart rate.

"Everyone was really excited," said Ian. "We realized, it's going to come down to Steve! On the other hand, everyone is terrified. This is going to come down to Steve!"

"I thought I was going to die," said Jan Aponavicius. "I was so nervous I thought I'd fall over and die."

Then, Navy called time-out. In football jargon, this is called, "icing the kicker," when the opposing team calls time-out for the sole purpose of trying to psych-out the place kicker. According to trainer Steve Bushee, the BC coaches and players believed this would not work on young Sid Vicious.

"We were all laughing because you can't ice this kid," said Bushee. "They call time out and he's just looking around, taking it all in like, golly gee whiz, I can't believe I'm standing on the sideline with my name on my uniform."

Johnny Ayers agreed.

"They're trying to freeze him and Steve just jogs over and I think he just thought it was La-La Land," Ayers said. "I don't know how he was able to do it but he seemed so calm."

In fact, as Director of Athletics, Gene DeFilippo, remembered it, Steve welcomed the time-out. "He said that was great they did that," said DeFilippo. "He was having trouble with the spot so that gave him time to pat down the ground."

Steve's teammates were far from calm. But they were confident.

"They were all saying, 'You've got this! No problem. You've done this a million times,'" said Steve.

Coach Spaziani, however, just stared straight ahead and didn't say a word.

So, as the players held hands on the sidelines, the fans at home and in the stands clutched each other and held their breath, Steve jogged back out into position. As the announcers noted, if he completed the thirty-seven-yard attempt, this would be the longest field goal of Steve's career.

Finally, the moment arrived. Jack Geiser snapped the ball to holder Chris Crane and Steve kicked the ball straight and hard, right down the middle. It was good!

With no time left, the Eagles won it, 25-24.

Chapter Ten

Resolve

As the Eagles players ran to midfield and mobbed Sid Vicious before hoisting him onto their shoulders, the BC fans in the stands celebrated wildly.

"Steve kicks the winning field goal and the whole place explodes!" said Steve's brother-in-law, Jamie. "Of course everybody knows who we are because we have these obnoxious signs. So the place goes bananas and people are shouting at us. We were screaming and our kids just burst out crying."

Steve's nephews, Tyler and Bradley, who were just four and six years old at the time, were most likely the only unhappy people in the stadium at that moment. Besides, of course, the dejected Midshipmen.

Matt Ryan, who had completed twenty of twenty-nine passes for 242 yards and one touchdown, forgot all about the frustration he felt prior to the winning kick.

"During the last play of the game, I was at the far end of the field and Matt was next to me on a knee," said Jay Civetti, the coach who discovered Steve kicking alone on the field the year before. "Steve kicked the thing and Matt jumped on my back and was slapping me saying, 'Steve did it!' Then we started sprinting to the field."

"I remember Matt was just pounding me in the chest," said Steve. "We were all jumping up and down and ended up in the endzone. Then they carried me to midfield. We had to stay there to get the trophy."

"That game was probably my worst game in college," said Jamie Silva. "I was getting so banged up, bruised up, beat up. I'd never been on the ground so much. So when the clock was winding down, I was just standing on the sidelines waiting for this to happen. Steve was running out there and I had all the faith in him. Then he put it through.

Ahh! It was such a relief off my back and I'm speaking as one of ninety guys on the team. I'm sure it was the same for everyone. Then we put him up on our shoulders. It was awesome."

"I can still see it," said Coach Frank Spaziani, who after the game, had a perfect (one-for-one) record as a head coach. "You couldn't draw that kick to be kicked any better. It was the perfect ending."

Incredibly, the kick was not only Steve's longest to date, but it won the game as time ran out. The win gave the Eagles a total of ten victories, a mark not met since Doug Flutie played at BC in the mid-1980's.

"I was just getting used to playing football for the first time so from my point of view, the whole year was just so fun," said Steve. "Plus we won ten games. No more than a handful of teams do that. We had a great season and it ended in an amazing fashion."

As the team collected their trophy and Steve collected accolades, there was another positive—although unexpected-- outcome to The Meineke Car Care Bowl game win. On the afternoon of the game, Moe Maloney, BC's former baseball coach (1988-1998), headed to the Newton Elks Lodge just outside of Boston to watch the game. Maloney, who had been coordinating charitable programs involving BC athletes as Assistant Director of the Neighborhood Center ever since he'd retired from coaching, had gotten to know Steve very well.

"I met him at one of my programs," said Maloney. "And he became an all-star as far as volunteering. He would come up and sit with me at basketball and hockey games. We became very friendly."

So, as a friend of Steve's and a hard-core fan of BC sports, not surprisingly, Maloney was engrossed in the game. But, as the afternoon went long, Maloney confronted a dilemma.

"I was in the process of giving up smoking," said Maloney. "I hadn't had a cigarette in two days. But I couldn't watch a game without beer or cigarettes. I always go to 4:00 mass and I couldn't drink beer before church. So I smoked some cigarettes."

Then, in the final seconds of the game, things got interesting.

"I said to myself, if that freakin' Stevie A, a walk-on, can kick this field goal then I can quit smoking," said Maloney. "Then I said it out loud to the guys in the bar, 'If he gets this field goal, I'm never smoking again!'"

Steve made the field goal and according to Maloney, he never had another cigarette. He did however have a couple of beers that day.

"I was late to Mass," he said. "It would have been 4:20 by the time I got there so I stayed at the Elks and started drinking."

After the 2006 season, Steve was presented with many awards and honors. Along with five other BC players, Josh Beekman, James Marten, Larry Anam, Ty Hall and Nick Larkin, Steve was named to the thirty-seven member 2006 All-ACC Academic Football Team. (To be considered, a player must have earned at least a 3.0 grade point average for the previous semester and maintained a cumulative 3.0 average during his academic career). He was also named to the espn.com all-bowl team.

Back at BC, at the all-sports banquet, he was honored with The Boston College Leadership Award, which Matt Ryan won the previous year, and BC's student newspaper, *The Heights,* named him 2007 Person of the Year.

Journalists and bloggers kept telling his story over and over, grouping his game-winning Meineke Bowl kick with the other great kicks in New England sports history such as Adam Vinatieri's Super Bowl kicks for the New England Patriots in 2002 and 2003 and David Gordon's forty-one yarder for BC that beat Notre Dame in the early 90's.

It seemed as if every day Steve was singled out by someone for what he had accomplished. He received numerous phone calls, letters and even a telegram from another former Boston College walk-on who played defensive back in 1991, State Representative Garrett Bradley (Third Plymouth District Massachusetts House of Representatives), whose advice to Steve was, "Enjoy it and be sure to take it all in."

To his astonishment, Steve was constantly recognized on campus and especially during football season, was repeatedly asked to sign autographs.

"It's just so strange for me to be doing that," Steve said, "But it's a lot of fun. I always think, people cannot really want my autograph. It takes so long to sign, too, with my last name, but I can never turn that down."

As always, his parents helped keep him grounded.

"I think he understands that it's like reality," Ben Aponavicius told *The Heights* after his son was named BC's Person of the Year. "You can fall just as fast as you can rise up."

One question Steve was constantly asked during his first season was whether he got nervous before those big kicks

"I don't remember ever being nervous for a kick," Steve said. "I got a lot more nervous watching something on tape or thinking about it after it happened. If I had missed one of those field goals against Virginia Tech or the clutch kick against Navy, I probably never would have played again. Things would have been a lot different if I'd missed those kicks."

After the season's thrilling conclusion, there was another question Steve was often asked. "What happens next year?"

Steve had played in every game since his stunning debut against Virginia Tech in October of 2006. And no one would soon forget the image of Sid Vicious being carried off the field in triumph following the bowl game win. His numbers weren't bad either; he'd made twenty-four of twenty-five PAT's and eight of eleven field goals the previous year. But what would happen next?

At that point, Steve was still a non-scholarship player. Coach O'Brien had discussed the possibility of upgrading Steve's status a few weeks before the end of the season, but Coach O'Brien was gone. A new head coach, the former Green Bay Packers offensive coordinator, Jeff Jagodzinski, had been hired, but the kicker and coach didn't know each other yet. Certainly Coach Jagodzinski, (a.k.a. "Coach Jags"), was familiar with Steve's story, but would that be enough?

Going into 2007, Steve definitely had some competition. It wasn't Ryan Ohliger. Although he performed kickoff duty for the last few games of the previous season, Ohliger had been declared academically ineligible prior to the Meineke Car Care Bowl. Then, in the Spring of 2007, following a hearing pertaining to the fight the previous October, Ohliger was suspended from school, and left soon after.

In 2007, Steve's competition would come from elsewhere. It was already common knowledge that kicker Billy Bennett of Torrey Pines High School in San Diego, would be heading to Chestnut Hill in the fall. Even before Steve came on the scene, Coach Petercuskie, who recently left to go to NC State with Coach O'Brien, had been tracking Bennett, who was one of the top high school kickers in the nation. Bennett, who routinely hit kicks from 44-51 yards during high school had also recently been rated the top kicker in the recruiting class by rivals.com.

Not only did Steve know that Billy Bennett was coming, but the two kickers had gotten to know each other when Billy stayed with Steve in the dorm during one of his two recruiting visits during the 2006 season.

So, as the upcoming season loomed, there were two questions on Steve's mind. Would he get a scholarship? And if he got a scholarship, with Bennett coming in, would he get the opportunity to play?

His answer, about the scholarship anyway, came in February of 2007.

"I was at a basketball game and I ran into our athletic director, Gene DeFilippo," said Steve. "I said hello to him and he said, 'So, how does it feel?' I said, 'How does what feel?' Then he said, 'To be on scholarship!' I think he thought the coaches had already told me. I said, 'Alright! Awesome!'"

According to DeFilippo, there wasn't any drama in the decision.

"I said, Aponavicius, as long as I'm here and you're here, you've got a scholarship," he said.

The next week, Steve was called into Coach Jagodzinski's office. It didn't take Steve long to realize that Coach Jags didn't know that Steve was already privy to the big news.

"He tried to make it all suspenseful," Steve said. "So, I played along with it."

The bottom line was that Steve had been granted a full scholarship, effective his junior year. This was more than a compliment and an honor for a student athlete. It was life-changing for his family who could now forego paying tuition for the next two years.

"The financial impact was incredible," said Steve's brother-in-law, Brian Reidy. "His parents would never have asked anybody to pay for his education but the fact that it happened, they were so grateful."

Even though the suspense regarding the scholarship was over, everyone was still left wondering who would be the starting kicker. Long before the first spring practice, Coach Jags told reporters, "A kicker is one of those guys who may be able to come in early and contribute as a freshman," he said. "But it's different kicking in front of 800 people and 8,000."

In other words, the coach wasn't saying. All he said was, "Let them compete."

When camp started that summer, Steve was listed as number one on the depth chart. The starting spot was his to lose.

"The year before I had nothing to lose and now I had everything to lose," said Steve.

As it turned out, when Coach Jags said, "Let them compete," he meant that literally.

"I had to fight for my job every single week," said Steve. "We'd have an open kicking competition and I'd have to go out and win the job. It was like kicking in a game five days a week. And there's a reason you only play twelve games in a year."

"In a year and a half, Steve went from being a fan to all of the sudden competing with the best nineteen-year-old kicker in the country," said Johnny Ayers. "Steve saw what a lot of kids in athletics see that he may not have seen before, and that's battling for a job."

Steve wasn't fighting for just any job. He was working to keep a spot on the roster of the Boston College Eagles, a team that in 2007 was one of the best in college football. One of the reasons for that was senior quarterback, Matt Ryan.

Going into 2007, Ryan was named pre-season ACC Offensive Player of the Year by several publications and hopes were high – there was even Heisman talk – despite the fact that he had played with an injured foot most of the previous year and had undergone surgery in the off-season. By all accounts he came to camp in top form and soon enough, he would be producing real results.

With Matt, who grew up in Exton, Pennsylvania, near Philadelphia, where he played quarterback for his high school, William Penn Charter, Steve once again found a Pennsylvania connection.

"We always used to talk about high school football in Pennsylvania," said Steve. "He went to a private school but he grew up close to some of the schools that played Easton. And we would talk about the Eagles and the Phillies and how being in Boston, we couldn't stand hearing about the Red Sox and the Patriots all the time. I've often wondered how it is for him now playing in the NFL. What do you do when you're a lifelong fan of one team and all of the sudden, you're on another team?"

As football fans know, Matt Ryan handled the dilemma just fine. After being drafted in the first round of the 2008 NFL draft, picked third overall by the Atlanta Falcons, he was immediately put to work and finished the year as 2008 NFL AP Offensive Rookie of the Year. The Falcons starting quarterback led his team to a 13-3 finish in 2010. All signs point to a Hall of Fame career. But back then, he was focused on winning games for Boston College.

"He's one of the few that didn't care at all about his ego; just about winning games," said Steve. "He was the nicest guy in the world but you'd see him sometimes just screaming at offensive linemen or yelling at a running back for missing a block. He definitely didn't put up with any sort of failure. You knew who was in charge. The coaching staff gave him a lot of freedom to change the play when he got to the line of scrimmage. He'd use hand signals and yell all sorts of stuff; the same kind of thing you see Peyton Manning doing on TV."

Matt had a winning attitude and leadership skills. He also had the goods.

"It was so neat just to watch him do stuff like seven-on-seven drills where there are no linemen and he's just throwing to receivers," said Steve. "The throws that he could make! I've still never seen a quarterback do some of the stuff that he did, like putting a ball three inches over a defender's head so it falls perfectly into place. Or getting it between two guys, over one guy and under the other guy. Or putting it on somebody's back shoulder when it needed to be there. Amazing."

A quarterback uses a very different skill set than that of a kicker.

"I've got so much more room to work with," said Steve. "I've got feet, he's got inches. And I can't imagine doing it when everything's moving, too. It's like he's playing a video game when he's playing. He's looking around, reading everything and processing things in three seconds that would take most people hours."

With Matt at the helm, and stand-out players including cornerback Dejuan Tribble; tight-end Ryan Purvis; running backs Andre Callender and L.V. Whitworth; left tackle Gosder Cherilus; safety Jamie Silva; linebackers Mark Herzlich and Jo-Lonn Dunbar; wide receivers Brandon Robinson and Kevin Challenger; and defensive tackle Ron Brace, the Eagles were looking at a very good football year.

As expected, the Eagles blasted out of the gates that season, winning their first eight in a row, including a last minute miracle win against Virginia Tech. But that's getting ahead of the story. First, BC had to play the season-opener at home against Wake Forest, a game in which Steve says he experienced perhaps his most embarrassing moment ever.

"I think it was the opening kickoff," he said. "The whole pre-season we had worked on just normal kickoffs, kicking it deep. Then, the first game comes and the coach says, you've got to squib it down the right sideline. I hadn't done it the whole previous month we were getting ready for the season. I dribbled one down the field; it went out of bounds so they took the five-yard penalty. I had to kick-off again. And I kicked the next one out of bounds! We had to move back to the twenty-yard line. Finally, I kept it in bounds. But later in the game, I kicked another one out of bounds. That was my first time getting booed by fans at home and in that case, I agreed with them."

Anybody can have a rough start; even Matt Ryan. His very first pass of the season was intercepted and run back for a touchdown. The team as a whole sputtered at the start. Before they knew it, the Eagles were down 21-0 during that first game and still managed to come back and win it (38-28).

"That really set the tone for the year," said Steve. "We knew that we could handle some adversity if we could come back from that without much trouble."

Indeed, from that point on, the Eagles were difficult to stop. After beating NC State (37-17), BC moved onto Georgia Tech, their third consecutive ACC opponent, and as it turned out, their third consecutive victory.

According to Steve, the Yellow Jackets' stadium in Atlanta is a great atmosphere in which to play a game and has the best playing surface in the ACC.

"It's one of the oldest on-campus college football stadiums in the country and it has a great view of downtown Atlanta," said Steve. "They have real grass and keep it incredibly short. It's flat like a fairway on a golf course."

It was also fun to play at Georgia Tech when No. 21-ranked BC bested a higher ranked (No. 15) team.

"I kicked an important field goal in the fourth quarter that took some momentum away from Georgia Tech who had scored 10 straight points on us," said Steve. "It put us up by two scores and after that we cruised. It wasn't a game-winning field goal but ones like that are just as satisfying. And much easier on my parents."

Several games into the season, the competition between the kickers for the starting position continued. Even though Steve remained the starting place-kicker, Bennett was frequently brought in for kickoffs and it was implied that anytime, he could take over for field goals. Especially the long ones. The pressure never let up.

"If you bring in a kid who can hit balls from sixty, sixty-plus yards, you're going to give him a shot right away even if you have (Sebastian) Janikowski on your team," said Johnny Ayers, who as the starting punter, was spared participation in the weekly kicking try-outs. "That's just good coaching. Steve was great until forty yards or so. Beyond that, he didn't really have the God-given leg to hit from forty-eight to fifty-four, which kind of separates really good college kickers from great college kickers. It's just eight yards. But Billy had that.

"He would bomb the ball in kickoffs, but week in and week out, Steve would beat him hash to hash. If you can hit kicks from the twenty-five yard line, which would be a forty-two-yard field goal, you're going to win a lot of games for your team. That's what Steve could do. You get the ball inside the twenty and Steve's going to hit the field goal. That was something Billy couldn't consistently do."

Despite the criticism that he struggled on longer kicks, Steve kicked his career-long field goal of forty-five yards during BC's 55-24 win over Bowling Green the first Saturday of October.

"I finally hit one over forty yards, so that's a monkey off my back," a smiling Steve told a reporter after the game.

Next, the Eagles headed to Notre Dame, a place where every college football player dreams of playing. Steve was no exception. But then the Eagles arrived in South Bend and he stepped out onto the hallowed ground of Notre Dame's field.

"The tradition there is amazing," said Steve. "Some of the people who have played on that field are some of the best players ever. But it's kind of tough to think about that when you're playing. I hate that field because they won't cut the grass. All I could think about was, I wish I had a lawnmower right now or at least a pair of scissors so I can cut this grass. It was so hard to kick!"

According to Steve, when he approached the ball to make his first kick, the ball looked like it was half under and half above ground.

"It was like hitting a golf ball out of the rough," he said. "I had to go into the grass to hit it."

As a result, he caught too much ground, his momentum was slowed and the ball sailed wide left.

Not only did he miss the kick, but a huge chunk of grass lodged between the sole and the rest of his shoe, causing it to split open. The trainers had to tape his shoe back together.

"You'd think the most profitable football program in the country could re-sod their field every once in a while," said Steve. "There are holes all over the field and it's uneven, with patches of different colors. I thought it was embarrassing that they had a field like that. Maybe it has something to do with trying to slow down their opponents."

Despite the conditions, BC beat their longtime major Catholic college rival (24-17) for the seventh consecutive time. For the first time since 1942, the Eagles were 7-0 and ranked No. 3 in the nation.

After the road trip to Notre Dame, the Eagles traveled to Blacksburg for a showdown against ACC rival Virginia Tech (at 6-1, ranked No. 11). Because Billy Bennett was sidelined with back problems, which he struggled with on- and -off all season, Steve handled both kick-offs and place kicks against the Hokies. (In fact, Bennett would be suspended from the team in 2008, first, due to academic ineligibility and later, for breaking team rules. He did not return to the team and soon after, left Boston College). As it turned out, this particular game became synonymous, at BC anyway, with the word "comeback".

The Hokies dominated the game until the last two-plus minutes, when Matt Ryan threw two touchdown passes in quick succession. First came a ninety-one scoring drive, capped off by a sixteen-yard touchdown pass to Rich Gunnell. Then, BC recovered an onside kick – the first onside kick that Steve had ever attempted-- at its own thirty-four-yard line and Ryan went back to work, clinching the win with a 24-yard touchdown pass to Andre Callender with eleven seconds left.

For the BC players on the sideline, the first fifty-five minutes of the game passed by incredibly slowly.

"The comeback was amazing, but the game was the worst," said Steve. "It was probably forty degrees and raining the whole game. I kicked the opening kickoff, then I didn't do anything for three and a half hours when all of the sudden I had to kick an extra point, an onside kick and another extra point. The hardest thing is trying to keep your leg loose during that long stretch of down time."

Football fans are familiar with players riding stationary bikes on the sidelines to stay warm. Steve only did this once and it was during that particular game.

"I was wearing one of those huge sideline jackets with the hood up over my helmet and riding the bike," said Steve. "I must have looked like such a loser."

Unfortunately for Steve, his bike ride didn't escape the notice of the Hokie faithful.

"There were people yelling at me the whole game, but you have to get used to that on the road," said Steve. "Mostly, it's pretty hilarious. But you wouldn't believe what people would say. Things like, 'You suck!' or when I kicked into the net, 'That one missed!' Also, a lot of things I can't repeat. I'd turn around and see some guy yelling at me. Here's a forty-year-old guy with a family yelling obscenities at some kid. I mean, what does his wife think?"

Although the Eagles lost the next two games, to Florida State and Maryland, which squelched their hopes for a national title, they finished the regular season with two big wins against Clemson and Miami.

The win over Clemson (20-17), which meant that BC was ACC Championship-bound, was another last-minute, come-from behind thriller. Steve hit two key field goals, one a forty-yarder in the second quarter and another, a twenty-yarder in the fourth.

"From where we stood that second field goal looked like it went wide right," said Steve. "The holder, Chris Crane, put his head down thinking I missed it, but it kind of slid back and went in. I had to pat him on the head and say, 'Hey, it went through.'"

Besides that crucial field goal, what Steve remembers most from the game, besides the sea of orange-wearing fans at Death Valley, was the noise. And the silence.

"That was the loudest game in college football history (132.8 decibels) and even at the game, when I was kicking, I couldn't hear anything," he said. "I'd always heard baseball players say that while they were at the plate during the World Series or basketball players when they were shooting a foul shot, that they heard nothing. I thought, how is that possible? But it really happens like that. For every field goal, time just stood still."

Chapter Eleven

In Stride

Eagles fans and the players who played on the squad that year won't soon forget the season of 2007.

"There was such a buzz on campus all season," said Steve. "After the Virginia Tech game, it was so unbelievable that we won it. It was a Thursday night game and when we got back at 4:00 AM there were probably two thousand kids lining the road in front of the stadium to meet us. Apparently the whole school just spilled out onto the campus and they had been celebrating all night. It felt like the whole year was like that."

BC's loss (30-16) during the ACC Championship game, which was essentially a re-match with a very fired-up, revenge-seeking Virginia Tech, was an enormous disappointment. ("That one still hurts," said Steve).

Still, the Eagles finished the season ranked tenth in the AP Top 25 and went out on a high note, beating Michigan State (24-10) in the Champs Sports Bowl in Orlando. The victory extended BC's bowl game winning streak, the longest in the nation, to eight. The win also meant that BC had won eleven games for the first time since 1940.

Once again, Steve was named to the All-ACC Academic Football Team, this time along with teammates Anthony Castonzo, Mark Herzlich, and Nick Larkin.

And although it was bittersweet to see them go, seven graduating seniors from the 2007 Eagles went on to play in the NFL. Gosder Cherilus and Matt Ryan, were first round draft picks. DeJuan Tribble was drafted in the second round and Jamie Silva, Jo-Lonn Dunbar, and Tyronne Pruitt signed contracts as free agents.

It's always difficult for fans to see talented players move on, but such is the nature of college football. The good news is that there are always fresh-faced rookies to take their place. In 2008, one of these rookies was punter Ryan Quigley, a standout high school punter and kicker from Little River, South Carolina (North Myrtle Beach).

During his senior year of high school, Ryan was named 2007 Statewide Special Teams Player of the Year by the South Carolina Football Coaches

Association. He also earned 2007 Associated Press All-State honors as a punter and captured Class 3A All-State and All-Region accolades in 2005, 2006 and 2007. His achievements had caught the attention of BC coaches and during the 2007 season, he made a recruiting trip to The Heights.

It was late December, just after the regular season had ended, when Ryan visited Chestnut Hill for his official visit. According to BC tradition, recruits don't stay in a hotel. Instead, they stay on campus in a dorm room with a current member of the football team. Ryan's host was Steve Aponavicius.

"I knew who Steve was," said Ryan. "The first time I ever heard of him, I was a junior in high school watching the BC-Virginia Tech (2006) game. I grew up a big Notre Dame fan and I couldn't stand BC. They always ruined Notre Dame's season! So I wasn't cheering for BC that night. But I was watching and then this kid's picture pops up on the screen. He's got this wild hair and I thought, wow, this guy is a clown. But he had a great smile. Then they tell the story of his first game and he went out there and knocked them all through. Any kicker watching that night thought it was pretty awesome. I couldn't wait to meet him."

When Ryan arrived on campus, Steve met him at Yawkey Athletic Center to show him around.

"Steve walks over to me and my mom wearing his normal, casual clothes," said Ryan. "It was real cold so he was all bundled up. He had this crazy hair. Like he had just rolled out of bed. The coaches were giving him a hard time, saying, 'You couldn't dress up for your guest?'"

Recruits aren't always paired with fellow position players. But often, kickers and punters end up together. This was true in Ryan's case and ultimately, it helped convince him to attend BC.

"Steve really let me know what was going on and what to expect," said Ryan. "Right off the bat, he was the nicest kid. It's probably one of the main reasons I went to BC."

According to Ryan, Steve plainly stated his case to the young recruit.

"He told me, 'If you don't come here, I'll have to punt and I suck at punting so you better get your butt here.'"

As it turned out, there was another factor in Ryan's decision to commit to the school. A day or so after he arrived in Chestnut Hill, an enormous snowstorm was forecast to hit the northeast. As a result, the dozen or so other recruits also on campus that weekend ended up leaving early to beat the storm. Only Ryan Quigley stayed.

Traditionally, the coaches take all the recruits and their parents out for a fancy dinner at the end of their official visit and this weekend was no exception. But this particular Saturday night, the lone dinner guests were Ryan Quigley and his mother. Steve came along, too.

"We went to The Capital Grill and it was our entire coaching staff and their wives," said Steve. "Then it was just me, Ryan and his mom. We had the reservation so we weren't going to cancel the dinner. We racked up this enormous bill, just to recruit one punter."

"Just me, Steve, and all this steak and lobster," said Ryan. "It was crazy. We couldn't eat it all. We still laugh about it."

Although he was recruited as a punter who averaged 46.1 yards per punt during his high school senior year, Ryan was also a place-kicker. This meant he was Steve's direct competition. In fact, the coaches began using Ryan for some kickoffs during his freshman year at BC, sometime after Billy Bennett left the team midway through the 2008 season.

"When I came to BC, I could punt and kick-off and kick field goals – kind of—but I was a pretty bad (place) kicker when I arrived," said Ryan. "I never gave Steve any trouble there. The thing was, we always cheered for each other. I never wanted him to do badly and he felt the same about me. It was whoever had the best day. We were happy for each other."

According to Steve, "It worked out great. He became one of the best punters that BC ever had."

In an ideal world, kickers stick together. On game day, you'll often see them standing next to each other on the sidelines or taking their warm-up kicks.

"We kind of had our side where we'd hang out," said Ryan. "Then, if one of us had a bad kick, the other one would come over. Steve knew not to say too much to me; I usually like to be pretty quiet and focused. But he'd say one thing and it would lift my spirits and we'd go back to focusing on the next kick. I'd do the same for him. But Steve was never the nervous guy. I was always the nervous wreck. I was more serious. Steve? I've never seen a guy so calm."

Athletic Director Gene DeFilippo was surprised to find out how composed the Eagles' kicker could be. Even during a moment of extreme pressure.

"During every game, when it gets to be three minutes to go, I always come out of the press box and go down on the field with the team, win or lose," said DeFilippo. "One particular game, I'm standing there and I know Steve is about to be called out for a field goal so I don't want to go near him. I just stand by myself and he starts to walk down near me. So, I move a couple steps down the other way and he moves towards me again. I move away. Finally, he comes and stands directly next to me and says, 'Coach, I'm getting really hungry. We've got to get this game over with.' Then he goes out and kicks the field goal and it wins the game. I'm thinking to myself, I can't tell anybody what he just said. I couldn't believe how cool he was."

Steve's even-keel personality and cool demeanor would serve him well during the fall of 2008. According to Steve, he struggled with missed kicks all season long. Ironically, most of his misses seemed to occur at home.

"I hit the same left post in the same endzone four times that season," said Steve. "It was the left post in the north endzone. I just couldn't believe it."

The home field advantage is well known in the world of sports and as much as Steve loved playing at Alumni Stadium, over and over again, it proved to be a challenging place for him to kick.

"Our stadium is far and away the windiest, coldest stadium in our division," said Steve. "It's not an easy place to kick. I think that year I missed six at home and zero on the road. My percentage at away games was much better than at home. So it was actually a treat to go on the road."

When a kicker starts to miss, he often starts to rethink everything he knows to be true about the simple act of kicking. Instead of just going with the flow he begins to question himself about the moment of impact and where, when or even if the laces of his shoe should hit the laces of the football. Instead of simply letting his leg glide through its natural arc he starts to think about acceleration and rotation and backspin.

As Steve remembers, he definitely fell into the trap of over-thinking things. At one point during that particular season, he says he actually forgot how to kick.

"I had just missed four of my last five field goals, two against Notre Dame and two against Clemson the week after that," said Steve. "Both home games. I was thinking way too much. I just couldn't do it."

"He took everything so to heart," said Don Yanowski, Eagles' special teams coach during the 2007 and 2008 seasons. "If he wasn't successful, he didn't really care about himself, he cared that he let the team down or that he let me down."

If Coach Yanowski thought Steve had let the team down, he didn't let on to Steve.

"I owe a lot of credit to Coach Yanowski," said Steve. "Without him, I don't know how I would have made it through that year. He was awesome. He always had a lot of confidence in me even in the beginning when I didn't have much experience under my belt. He was always a big supporter of mine."

According to Jamie Silva, Steve's teammates were also constant and consistent supporters of their kicker.

"There was a time when he was kind of down," said Jamie. "But we reminded him that we all had faith in him and that he was there for a reason. He got there the hard way. He ended up beating out a scholarship guy for a reason."

Steve's roommate, Kevin Murphy, remembers the nights following a few games where Steve missed one or more than one of his kicks.

"There were a couple of games when I had Steve suicide watch going on," said Murph. "(As equipment manager) I had to work late so I'd make it a point to go back to the room and check on him, then go back to work. He was really hard on himself but then he'd realize he wasn't the sole reason we'd lost a game. There were hundreds of plays that determined the final outcome. He'd get down but he'd usually get over it quickly. If he was in a funk, it usually didn't carry over until the next day."

Mostly, after a miss or a loss, Steve got back to work. During every practice, he made it a point to always keep busy and stay on task.

"You have to work hard to get your teammates respect," Steve said. "There are a lot of times at practice where you're sitting around doing nothing and then if you miss a kick on Saturday, they're going to remember you sitting around doing nothing. If you're out there working on your steps or putting in extra work kicking, they'll remember that you put your time in. You always hear that kickers don't do anything. They don't work hard. You can't kick during the entire two and a half hours of practice, but there are some little things you can always do to get better."

So, the season went on. As the Eagles suited up for the Florida State game, Steve didn't know whether or not he was going to play. Then, ten minutes before kickoff, he got the nod from Coach Jags.

During that game, something finally clicked. Not only did Steve successfully kick two field goals during the Eagles' 27-17 victory over the Seminoles, but somehow he also turned a corner as a kicker. From that game on, he didn't miss a kick for the rest of the season, going six-for-six for the last several games. In fact, Steve made every kick – except for one – for the remainder of his career.

Like dozens of successful kickers that came before him, Steve thrived when he tuned out the chatter, from the trash talk of opposing linemen ("I'm gonna break your leg, kicker…We're gonna run you right over…") to the rantings of bloggers, ("This guy sucks…BC needs a new kicker…"). Steve was his own worst critic and he knew he had to turn deaf ears to the criticisms of himself and others and most of all, learn to put the immediate past behind him. He needed to develop what coaches or broadcasters refer to as "a short memory."

According to fellow-kicker Ryan Quigley, Steve accomplished that goal and inspired him to do the same. "Steve was always able to forget about the last kick and keep his mind clear," said Ryan. "He helped teach me that."

A kicker needs to be able to forget what he's already done and completely focus on the task at hand. Steve knew this and adopted a routine where prior to every kick, he thought only about what needed to be done at that moment. Then, briefly, just prior to taking his steps, he would tap the brakes.

"I used to write the words, 'Be Smooth,' on my left hand with a Sharpie before every game," said Steve. "It was a reminder to slow down. On the average field goal, you want to kick at about eighty percent of your full strength. I'd look at my hand before I kicked to remind myself to slow down and not run at the ball too quickly. When I was smooth, everything was in line and I had more success. During my conversations with Johnny Ayers I came to the conclusion that I kicked a lot better when I wasn't trying so hard."

"He stuck with it and figured it out," said Johnny. "It's a testament to him as a kicker and to his growth as a mental athlete."

Thinking too much can be dangerous for a kicker or any player especially when he starts identifying and trying to repeat certain lucky patterns. We've all heard about the ball player who won a big game after eating a chicken dinner and then ate only chicken for the rest of the season.

Then there are stories we try to ignore, such as the ones about the players who refuse to wash their lucky socks or underwear while in the midst of a winning streak.

Even though he admits to always putting on his left shoe before his right shoe and his right pant leg before his left pant leg, Steve says he tried to steer clear of superstitions.

"I tried to avoid them at all costs because they can really overtake you in a position like kicker," Steve said.

Still, there were certain routines Steve adhered to. The most important of these involved his shoes.

"I had this one model of cleats that I liked kicking with," said Steve, "and Reebok, our sponsor only made it for one year. It was a thin, leather soccer cleat. Later, I tried new cleats but I just couldn't kick in them so I had to tape the left one up because it was absolutely falling apart."

Steve also liked to wear wristbands, those colorful silicone gel bands such as the ones made popular by Lance Armstrong's Livestrong campaign. During every game, Steve wore two of them -- one for the Easton Red Rovers and one for the BC Eagles.

"Halfway through my last season the Rovers band fell apart," said Steve. "It was red when I got it and by the time it broke all the color had rubbed off. I'd worn it in every game I'd ever played in so I was kind of upset when it broke."

As the 2008 season drew to a close, Steve wondered whether or not his luck had run out. He was a senior, and although he'd been on the team for four years, he only played for three so he had another year of eligibility left. He wanted to play another season and planned to take graduate courses at Boston College if he stayed. But ultimately, it was up to the head coach. Would it be best for the team to give a scholarship to a veteran or would the Eagles be better served bringing in and developing a young kicker? As BC traveled to Nashville to take on Vanderbilt in the Music City Bowl, their last game of the season, Steve still didn't know his fate.

Then, in early January, Coach Jags was fired after he interviewed for a position with the New York Jets. Soon after, it was announced that the new head coach would be longtime defensive coordinator, Frank Spaziani, who had served as interim head coach during the Meineke Car Care Bowl of 2006, the game where Steve kicked the last second, game-winning field goal against Navy. Coach Spaz would never forget that moment and the first win it brought him as a head coach. More importantly, he knew Steve well and believed in him as a player.

No question, Steve's numbers were good. If he played, he would enter the 2009 season as the ACC's active leader in career field goals (34) and PAT's (107).

"There really was no decision," said Spaziani, "unless he didn't want to come back. That was the only conversation we had."

So, Steve stayed and played for another year. His final season would turn out to be memorable indeed.

As the team would find out soon enough, life under Coach Spaziani was reminiscent of life under Coach Tom O'Brien, who had brought Coach Spaz with him as an assistant when O'Brien came to BC as head coach in 1997.

"Coach Spaz's style is similar to Coach O'Brien's style," said Steve. "It's a no-nonsense kind of deal. He doesn't mess around. We're required to go to class. He doesn't tolerate failure. He's like an old school football coach. He played for Coach Joe Paterno at Penn State, so it's that kind of mentality."

Spaziani, who grew up in Clark, New Jersey, was an ace pitcher and quarterback in high school. At Penn State, he played running back and defensive end on the football team. After graduation, he stayed on as a graduate assistant on Paterno's staff. His first coaching job was working for Coach George Welsh at The Naval Academy, where Spaziani coached tight ends and tackles, and later coached defensive backs. While at Navy he also met and worked with another young coach, Tom O'Brien.

According to a Boston Globe story, Spaziani, O'Brien, and another young coach, Art Markos, used to go out together in Annapolis where O'Brien and Markos would tell girls that Spaziani was Tony Orlando. A few of them even believed it.

After his stint at Navy, Spaziani worked on Welsh's staff at the University of Virginia for nine years, then served as defensive coordinator for pro teams in Canada (Winnipeg and Calgary) for five years before coming to BC. Twelve years later, he took the reins as boss.

Although he coached running backs for two years when he first came to BC back in 1997, Spaziani spent the majority of his pre-head coaching seasons plotting defensive strategies for the Eagles. Accomplishments on BC's defensive side over the years include a rush defense ranked first in the Big East in 2004 and first in the ACC in 2005. In 2007, Spaziani's overall defense was ranked second in the nation and led the ACC in rushing defense, allowing just 75.5 yards per game. The BC defense also was ranked second in the ACC in red zone defense that year.

In 2008, the Eagles were ranked in the Top Ten in the nation in seven defensive categories and the outlook for the 2009 season was promising, mostly due to the return of several outstanding veterans, including the player who would step into the spotlight in a major way that year—senior linebacker, Mark Herzlich.

In May of 2009, several months before the season's start, Herzlich, who was named 2008 ACC Defensive Player of the Year, shocked his new head coach and teammates when he disclosed that he had been diagnosed with Ewing's Sarcoma, a rare form of cancer most often found in bone or soft tissue. Doctors gave the young athlete a 70% chance of survival and told him he would never play football or even be able to run again.

"It was unbelievable," said Steve. "He played in the spring game and then a couple of days later went to the doctor and found out he had cancer. My heart just sank. To think that this guy could be gone was unthinkable. The guy was Superman! He could do anything. The stuff he did on the field every week was incredible. He was on top of the world and could have been a top-round pick in the NFL draft that year but he decided to come back to school and stick it out for another year. Then he got sick. It was amazing. He was one of the best athletes in the country. If it could happen to him, it could happen to anybody."

That spring, Herzlich left school and returned home to Philadelphia where he underwent aggressive treatment, including months of intense chemotherapy and the insertion of a twelve-inch titanium rod to reinforce his left leg.

Incredibly, Herzlich, who said he constantly visualized himself once again running through the Alumni Stadium tunnel with his team, was back on campus in early August. Although he sat out the season, he was back attending classes and as many football practices as possible while he continued his treatment in Boston.

In early October, when BC was set to play Florida State at home, ESPN's College Game Day came to The Heights for the big match-up and interviewed Herzlich on the stage prior to the game.

"That's when he announced that he was cancer-free," said Steve. "It was awesome to watch; there were a lot of big, tough guys tearing up. It was so unbelievable. He went from diagnosed to cancer-free in just over seven months."

According to Steve, Herzlich's illness turned into a major positive.

"There was such an outpouring of support, not just from us but from the entire ACC," said Steve. "All year, every team we played donated a big check and they collected helmets and jerseys for raffles. It was really a rallying point for the entire conference. It was really cool to be a part of it, especially since the ending to the story is so good."

Indeed, the story had a truly happy ending. Herzlich returned to the team in 2010. He started all thirteen games and finished the year with sixty-five tackles and four interceptions. As of July 2011, he is NFL-bound after signing with the New York Giants as a free agent.

BC fans, and every football fan who was touched by his story, will be watching.

Chapter Twelve

The Record

Every college football team develops its own traditions and rituals over the years and Boston College is no exception. Among the Eagles' unique traditions is The Eagle Walk, established during the 2007 season, when two hours prior to every home game, the team gathers in front of Corcoran Commons with the band and cheerleaders and marches across campus all the way to the Yawkey Center as fans, students and alumni line the streets and cheer them as they pass.

For the players, the third of a mile march is an adrenaline rush and a great chance to see and talk to fans, such as one of Steve's favorite fans turned friend, Charlie McLaughlin, better known as The Duke.

"I'd talk to Steve before every game," said The Duke. "Then I'd sit in the endzone and pray for him to make his kicks."

Another cherished ritual for Eagles players is the pre-game speech given by various coaches and assistant coaches, usually when the team is gathered in the hotel the night before games. Now into his fourth year as a player, Steve had heard many of these speeches. Some of the best came from Associate Athletics Director for Football Operations Barry Gallup, who back when he was a student athlete at BC in the 1960's became the greatest receiver in BC history and has since logged some thirty years in various roles at Boston College.

"Coach Gallup is our resident historian, really," said Steve. "His speeches are unbelievable. We're ready to run through a wall after he speaks. He spoke before we played Florida State one time and even though we were huge underdogs, we still won. I think we're 12-0 on games where he speaks."

Gallup takes little credit for his winning streak.

"I like to motivate people," he said. "I always kid Coach Spaz, 'You've got to give me a big game!' Usually I get the Parents Weekend game or a game we were supposed to win anyway."

The Eagles won their fair share of games during the 8-5 season of 2009, beginning with lop-sided victories over Northeastern and Kent State. Then, after losing to Clemson, BC came back during the next game to beat Wake Forest in overtime (27-24). Wins over Florida State (thank you, Coach Gallup), and NC State soon followed.

Whether his team was winning or losing, there were some powerful back stories at Boston College that year. There was Mark Herzlich's inspiring comeback and the unexpected debut of quarterback Dave Shinskie, a twenty-five-year-old freshman who graduated from high school and spent several years pitching in the minor leagues before coming to Boston College. And once again, there was the story of Sid Vicious. No longer a rookie, the kicker had become a veteran and as the Eagles worked their way down the schedule, game after game, it seemed as though he could not miss.

Partly, his consistency and confidence stemmed from the fact that during his final season, he knew his job was secure. There were no more kicking competitions-- those left with Coach Jags.

His new special teams coach, Mike Dawson, had faith in him and pretty much left his kicker to his own devices.

"Steve's very intelligent and he's a student of his craft," said Dawson. "He knew when he was right, when he was wrong and how to fix it. I'd give him input to keep him on track as far as work-outs and that kind of thing, but I didn't mess around with his technique. I just let him stay consistent with what he was doing."

According to Steve, his head coach also trusted him to do his job without too much input.

"Coach Spaz was awesome," Steve said. "He would come over and talk to me all the time but it would never be about kicking. He'd never say, 'I want you to do this instead of that.' He'd say, 'What did you do this weekend?' He had a great approach with kickers and people in general."

By his fourth year, Steve had learned the ropes and knew how to do his job on the field. Regarding the rough and tumble part of the game, he knew how to avoid getting hit after a kick or when to take a hit and garner a penalty for his team or when he should simply fall down after a kick to stay out of harm's way. On the sidelines, he had become accustomed to the waiting game a kicker has to play, finding a way to stay warm and ready despite the constant stops and starts during a football Saturday.

"When we had the ball, if we got past mid-field, I'd go warm up and kick a few balls into the net," said Steve. "I'd try not to kick more than two or three balls because you can end up worn out from warming up too much. It's really hard on your body to warm up and cool down over and over. I'd be so sore on Sundays just from standing for four hours and warming up and cooling down. Sometimes I could barely get out of bed. I'd get a lot of grief for being a kicker and being so sore."

Warming up and cooling down is something a kicker does mentally as well as physically.

"To me, that's the hardest thing for a specialist," said Coach Dawson. "You have to be mentally ready to kick at any moment. We might be at mid-field saying, 'Are you ready?' Then, the kicker kicks a bunch of practice balls and the drive stalls. You have to be really mentally strong."

As the season progressed, it became evident that Steve had found his rhythm in every aspect. Game after game, he was making all his kicks. Both home and away, every time he attempted a field goal or an extra point, he simply did not miss. And a funny thing happens when a kicker does that. He tallies up a lot of points. In fact, it soon occurred to Steve and others that as incredible as it was, he was on-pace to become Boston College's All-Time Leading Scorer.

Around the practice field and in the locker room, little mention was made of the fact that the walk-on known as Sid Vicious who got a chance to play, then thrived, then struggled, then became a four-year starter and thrived again, was closing in on the team record for total points scored (262 points) set by placekicker, Brian Lowe, back in 1989.

Much the same way they would leave a kicker alone before a big kick in a game, most of his teammates and coaches simply didn't talk about the record.

"It's not like people were avoiding him or anything," said trainer Steve Bushee. "It just wasn't a topic of conversation. No one would come in and say, 'Oh, just three more to go.' It was kind of unmentioned and business as usual. And as far as he was concerned, his routine didn't change. His attitude and the way he handled himself definitely didn't change. He was still just as humble as when he first walked in the door."

When people did ask him about the impending record, Steve would play it down, pointing out that there haven't been many four-year starting kickers at BC, so he had an edge in number of games played. He'd also say that he was fortunate to play on winning teams. (More touchdowns mean more opportunities to score extra points). He also pointed out that Lowe, the current record holder who also got his start as a walk-on, was ahead of him in number of field goals.

"When it was just me and him alone, I'd say, 'Man, you're definitely going to break that record,'" said Ryan Quigley. "But he'd say, 'I don't know. I just have to go out there and kick.'"

Steve's close friends and family were aware that he was getting close to breaking the record. Back in Easton, Pat McCutcheon had a countdown calendar on her refrigerator, tracking Steve's points. Sports reporters and bloggers took note of his escalating numbers and as Steve edged towards accomplishing his feat, stories began to appear in *The Boston Herald, The Boston Globe, The Express-Times,* as well as on various websites and blogs. One person who was definitely keeping close track of Steve's kicking tally was Kevin Murphy.

As equipment manager, among other things, Murph was responsible for retrieving the ball used during the record-breaking kick.

"That was crazy," said Murph. "I had to check up on him constantly. Is this the kick that breaks the record? Is this the one? I had to make sure that particular ball wasn't put back into the game. We definitely wanted to save that one."

Then, on Halloween of 2009, during BC's home game against Central Michigan, with 6:35 remaining in the third quarter, following Eagles running back Montel Harris' three-yard touchdown run, Steve took his steps and kicked the ball held by Billy Flutie, who was into his second season as the holder. The kick, his third extra point of the day, was good.

It was official. Steve Aponavicius was the top-scorer in BC history, with 263 points. Before the day was done, he notched an additional PAT and an eighteen-yard field goal, giving him a total of 267 points.

Even though BC's coaches mostly stuck to their script, saying any record was good if it helped the team, Coach Spaz couldn't help but chuckle during the post-game press conference.

"It's tremendous for Steve, it really is," he said. "He drops out of the student section and after a lot of hard work he becomes the all-time leading scorer."

Brian Lowe, who reporters noted was not given the benefit of his nine points in the 1986 Hall of Fame Bowl because at the time, the NCAA didn't recognize bowl stats, was gracious as his record was broken.

"I might have kept (the record) for another week," Lowe told reporters. "But that doesn't take away from what he's done. It's a great accomplishment. I'm happy for him."

Back in the locker room, Steve was awarded the game ball. Well, not exactly the game ball. But a game ball. The actual ball Steve used for the record breaking kick had been dutifully snatched up by Murph, who then stashed it in his desk for safe-keeping until it could be inscribed and presented to Steve at the team banquet at the end of the year.

Steve kept his tally going during the Eagles next several games. Incredibly, he didn't just hit some of his kicks. Deep into BC's November schedule, he was still hitting all of his kicks.

"His consistency was amazing especially on the extra points," said Jon Meterparel, the radio voice of the Eagles. "It's underrated. (People say) oh, an extra point, how difficult is that? But you realize how difficult it is when you see fifty or sixty percent of the kickers in the country will miss three or four extra points a year."

Even though he was a veteran and now, a record-holder, it was never a given that Steve, or any kicker, would sustain a streak like this. Looking back, Steve has some perspective on what went right.

"My whole mindset was different that last season," said Steve. "I knew it was my last year. In previous years, I'd really poured everything into football. I'd watch film of every team we played. I stopped doing that. I stopped over-thinking. Also, I got a great girlfriend."

Steve met his girlfriend, Taylor Peyton, a Boston College softball pitcher and nursing student in April of 2009. It was Marathon Monday, a major party day at The Heights, when classes are cancelled and students line Commonwealth Avenue to cheer as Boston Marathon runners make their way up what's known as Heartbreak Hill, the last major hurdle in the final six miles of the marathon.

Steve and Taylor first met at The Mods, a group of houses in the middle of campus where seniors live. Taylor knew who Steve was, but they had never talked to each other before, although Steve had sent her a Facebook friend request just a couple of weeks prior.

"I had thrown a no-hitter and Steve saw a story about it on the BC website," said Taylor. "He follows every sport. So, that's why he friended me."

Taylor accepted the friend request and forgot about it. Then, a few weeks later she met Steve in person and they hit it off, despite the fact that their first conversation was a disagreement about the privileged status of football players at Boston College.

"I made the point that girls' sports are valued differently than boys' sports," Taylor said. "He was trying to defend himself, which was a bad idea. I said, 'I'm sure you guys have the nicest locker room. You should see ours. We can all barely fit in there.' He said, 'It couldn't be that bad.' So I took him and showed him."

Figuring no one would be in the locker rooms on Marathon Monday, Taylor and Steve visited the girls' locker room where Steve admitted to being very surprised by the meager facilities. Then they went to the football locker room.

According to Taylor, "They had plasma TVs, Nintendo, leather chairs, a million pairs of shoes in each of their lockers. Someone had folded all their clothes. They even had Powerade machines! I gave him such a hard time."

Steve and Taylor are so competitive that they can't even play a game of darts against each other without it turning into something intense.

"We can't play against each other," said Steve. "We have to be on the same team. That's the only way."

A week or so after Steve and Taylor met, Steve's friend from Easton, Pete Cheng, came to visit. It was the weekend of BC's spring football game and Steve remembers being torn between wanting to be with Taylor and not wanting to abandon his friend.

"We did a lot of stuff together that weekend, just the three of us," said Steve. "Pete never took the hint that I really liked this girl! But he was the first of my friends to give her his stamp of approval so that meant a lot."

Looking back, Steve said that Taylor's presence completely changed his perspective during his final football season.

"A few years before, all I could think about was the next set of winter workouts or summer conditioning, or spring ball or the next season. Then I finally realized that there was a lot more to life than football because football was going to be over. Stepping back from it a bit really helped me in the mental side of the game. Suddenly, I was more concerned about where Taylor and I were going to dinner than if I made the third field goal in practice."

Steve told Taylor how different things were now that she was around.

"He said that in the past, if he missed a field goal he'd go sit in his room," said Taylor. "But I wasn't about to sit around and be depressed with him."

"Before, if I missed that last kick that's all I would think about until the next day," said Steve. "My last year, I totally stepped out of football practice when practice was over. I wish I would have done that sooner because it really helped me. I don't want to make it sound like I wasn't working hard, because I was. But it wasn't consuming me anymore. I wasn't on edge all the time. It made things so much easier."

Indeed, BC's kicker made things look easy during the Fall of 2009. After breaking the points scoring record, he methodically went about his business, kicking one successful kick after another. Going into the Eagles' final regular season game of the year, an ACC matchup against Maryland, Steve was the only perfect college kicker in the country.

Things started off well with Steve completing three field goals in the first half, including two in the final four minutes of the second quarter that gave BC a 16-10 lead. But then, during the third quarter, Steve set up for another field goal attempt. He connected with the ball and Eagles' fans, many of whom had come to expect perfection from their kicker, gasped as the thirty-one-yard kick went wide right, spoiling Steve's perfect season. Finally,

Sid Vicious missed one.

Soon enough, the kicker got another chance. BC was up by six when Steve nailed a forty-two-yard field goal, his longest of the season, which turned out to be hugely important when Maryland scored a late touchdown. By then, the game was out of reach. BC won it (19-17) and Steve had kicked a career high four field goals.

Steve finished the season thirteen for fourteen on field goals and thirty-seven for thirty-seven for PAT's. After his final game, his career total stood at 290 points and he was ranked first in BC history in field goal percentage (.734) and extra points made (149). He was ranked second in field goals (47), after Brian Lowe's total of 57.

Once again, Steve was named to the All-ACC Academic Football team, this time along with teammates Anthony Castonzo, Nathan Richman and Emmett Cleary. After receiving this honor following all of his active seasons, Steve became only the eleventh player in ACC history to win the award four times.

The numbers and achievements are remarkable. But they are even more extraordinary when put into context. A guy who never played organized football at any level gets discovered kicking field goals for fun. He walks-onto the team, a good team, known to be nationally-ranked, with no expectations that he will ever actually play in a game.

He gets a chance to play and performs perfectly during his first game, a high profile media event. He goes on to play in every game for the remainder of his first season and during every game for a full three years after that. Along the way, he wins a bowl game as time runs out, beats out the best young kicker in the country to keep his job and along the way, becomes the all-time leading scorer in the history of his school, all the while excelling academically. That's the story.

"What are the chances of all this happening?" said Jon Meterparel. "It was like there was a big script written someplace and someone connected the dots. It's nuts. All the lightning rod moments that he had. It's something you're never going to see again."

"If I had sat down and written how I would have liked everything to go, I never could have imagined this story," said Steve. "I couldn't have written a better script for how things played out."

When people hear a story like the one about BC's Sid Vicious, a guy who became "the people's kicker," they often say, "What a lucky guy." Steve heard that a lot.

"I realize that I was extremely lucky," said Steve. "I got a big break but I was ready for it. You really have to be ready to be lucky."

Not long after he walked-on to the team, Steve's uncle, Don Scrima, who like the rest of the family knew that Steve had spent years practicing field goals on his own, told him, "You're the definition of luck. And that's when preparation meets opportunity."

Besides lucky, the other term Steve heard often was "overnight success".

According to strength coach Todd Rice, "When Steve finally got his opportunity it was just like, Boom! But it was a long time coming, his overnight success. I think it had to do with his parents and him as a person. No coach had him out there kicking on the field turf when it was hot and sticky during the summer and doing all those things before he even joined the team. He acted like a scholarship kid the minute he got here."

Steve said he wouldn't trade any piece of the story for anything. The memories of waking before sun-up and walking in the freezing cold to practice or getting rocked on a brutal tackle during a kickoff against Michigan State are blended together in a positive collage of images that include the game-winning field goal against Navy as well as a fourth field goal to beat Maryland or an overtime kick to beat Wake Forest. Even the permanent, painful bruise he carries on his left foot after years of kicking through a thin, thin shoe, is a welcome reminder of his Sid Vicious days when it seemed as if nothing could wipe the smile from his face.

"He was always grinning," said strength coach, Jason Loscalzo. "He had a perma-smile going even when he was working out or under pressure. He just did his thing and enjoyed doing it."

As much as this story is about luck and perseverance, it's also about Boston College, a place where the football team excels despite having a smaller student body and due to high academic standards, a smaller pool of players to draw from each season.

Ultimately, the story of Sid Vicious is about family, the Aponavicius family, who watched as Steve excelled at every turn.

"In the beginning, we were all just thrilled that he was on the team," said Steve's sister, Kristin Kalbach. "That was plenty for us. If it never became more than just him standing on the sideline wearing a uniform, that would have been OK. Then all the rest of it came along. It kept blowing our minds."

Incredibly, his parents made the six-plus hour drive from Easton to Boston to attend every home game and barely missed a road game during the four years their son played at BC. Of course Ben Aponavicius was always more than a mere spectator.

"After I started playing, I'd go home to Easton for a couple of weeks every summer and my dad and I would go over to Lafayette College near our house after they got their new turf field," said Steve. "He'd complain about his hands hurting so I got him wide receiver gloves and he'd wear those to catch the field goals. It looked really funny to see a sixty-two-year-old guy out there with football gloves on, running around, catching the ball and punting it back to me. He doesn't know the first thing about kicking, but he'd watch me and tell me if I did something different this time or that – something I didn't do before.

"He made it his life, too. Both my dad and I had hours into it; kicking all that time over the years. My parents had everything to do with getting me where I got a chance to go."

And really, the Sid Vicious story is all about one guy taking a chance and seeing what he might accomplish. It's about being ready for your big break.

To think, it all could have been different. What if Steve had never taken his homemade tee and gone out to kick field goals during his first day at school? What if the grounds crew at Boston College had locked the stadium when it wasn't in use? What if it had rained that day or if Steve had met some friends and gone to eat instead of heading out to the field? What if the graduate assistant who approached him and asked him to join the team had taken a different route to his class that night?

"It all happened because one lucky day I was kicking balls for the hell of it when a coach walked by," said Steve. "If I got to the field twenty minutes later that day, my life could have been totally different."

* * *

*In June of 2009, Steve Aponavicius graduated from Boston College with
a degree in finance and marketing and received his MBA in December of 2010.
He lives in Southern California where he works for J.P. Morgan Chase.*

Thanks to all my family, coaches, teammates, and all the great friends who supported me along the way. Nothing would have been possible without you. – ***Steve Aponavicius***

Bibliography

Boston College Football Vault: The History of the Eagles,
by Reid Oslin (Whitman Publishing, 2008)

Boston College Media Guides (2005-2010)

History of Boston College: From the Beginnings to 1990, by Charles
F. Donovan, S.J., David R. Dunigan, S.J. and Paul A. FitzGerald,
S.J. (The University Press of Boston College, 1990)

Tales from the Boston College Sideline, by Reid Oslin
(Sports Publishing, L.L.C., 2004)

bc.edu
boston.com/bostonglobe
bostonherald.com
espn.com

Also: articles from *The Easton Express-Times, The Morning Call,*
Sports Illustrated, USA Today and *The Boston College Chronicle*

Cultures of the World: Lithuania, by Sakina Kagda (Marshall Cavendish, 1997)

Lithuania: The Rebel Nation, by V. Stanley Vardys and
Judith B. Sedaitis (Westview Press, 1997)

Easton PA: A History, by Richard F. Hope (Authorhouse, 2006)

Historic Easton, by Marie Summa, Frank Summa, and
Leonard Buscemi, Sr. (Arcadia Publishing, 2000)

"Sometimes stories that are too good to be true
are, stop the presses, actually true.
That is the case with Steve Aponavicius, field goal kicker from nowhere.
He is 'Rudy' times 10. Read M.B. Roberts sweetly written tale,
suck in that gut and take a shot at whatever dream you've deferred.
This, my friend, is your inspiration." *– Leigh Montville, award-winning sportswriter and author of bestselling books including, Ted Williams: The Biography of an American Hero*

"Steve started a revolution.
He had Average Joes all around the country walking onto
big programs thinking that they were going to become the
next star. What people didn't realize was that Steve was no
average Joe!" *– Jamie Silva, BC All-American and Indianapolis Colts safety*

"I've been around BC sports for a long time and
I think it's the greatest story that our school has ever produced.
This kid who never played organized football becomes the
leading scorer in the history of Boston College." *– Moe Maloney, Head Coach, Boston College Baseball (1988-1998)*

Made in the USA
Lexington, KY
05 December 2011